4-27-65 (63-11086)

BUILDERS OF THE NORTHWEST

BUILDERS
of the
NORTHWEST

By JALMAR
JOHNSON

With an Introduction by Stewart H. Holbrook
Illustrated

DODD, MEAD & COMPANY · New York

For Dorothy

INTRODUCTION

The Pacific Northwest was the last corner of the United States to be settled. The Northeast began permanent settlement in 1620. By then the Southeast was a long-established colony of Spain. The Southwest corner dates from long before the American Revolution. But the Northwest had nothing comparable to these populous places until the late 1840s, though it could boast of one lone trading post as early as 1811.

Thus the History that elsewhere required from two hundred to three hundred years for its unfolding was compressed into less than a century.

Events were to move swiftly in these parts. Our Blockhouse Era lasted only two years. It had passed by 1856. That was the end of the only genuine pioneers-Indian war fought in the Northwest. The later troubles with Indians were local uprisings and were put down by professional soldiers.

Nowhere else did the Blockhouse Era pass so quickly as it did here. Nowhere else, too, did the railroads arrive so late and begin to disappear so soon.

Within a period of thirty years, 1859–1890, Oregon, Washington, and Idaho were admitted as sovereign states to the Union.

In his account Mr. Jalmar Johnson has selected a dozen men and women who surely belong among our most purposeful pioneers, and they will do to indicate the many varied talents that came in the Covered Wagons and began almost at once to influence settlement in what was first known as The Oregon Country and became the Pacific Northwest.

There are names more widely familiar than those in Mr.

Johnson's book; but he has chosen wisely in order to present not a "typical" pioneer, if there *are* any such, but rather those who appeared at exactly the right time to act as needed by existing conditions. Taken all together, it seems to me the Author could hardly have chosen better.

STEWART H. HOLBROOK
Portland, Oregon

CONTENTS

ILLUSTRATIONS

BUILDERS OF THE NORTHWEST

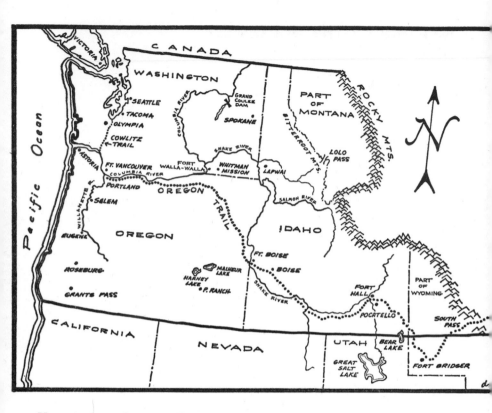

Vast territory between Rocky Mountains and Pacific Ocean and between
Canada and the northern boundaries of California, Nevada and Utah became
part of the United States in 1846 by agreement between the United States and
Great Britain. American settlers coming over the Oregon Trail (heavy dotted
line) by the South Pass won the country peacefully for the United States.
Early wagon trains stopped at the Whitman Mission, but after the Indian
massacre they passed through present northeast Oregon farther south. Explorers Lewis and Clark and Chief Joseph, in his strategic retreat, used Lolo
Pass through the Bitterroot Mountains. (*Portland Oregonian*)

PROLOGUE

Exactly thirty years before the first principal in this series of profiles stepped out on the stage, two sea captains—one American, the other British—began building the backdrop. They set the scene for a long, dramatic contest between the United States and Great Britain over the Pacific Northwest, an area larger than Texas.

Our first "actor" appeared in 1822. The scene-setting began in 1792, a year of vital importance to the whole continent of North America.

On April 27, Captain George Vancouver took a look from a distance at a couple of capes on the largely unexplored Pacific Coast. He was a British officer on his way in the sloop-of-war *Discovery* to negotiate with some Spaniards over control of Nootka Harbor on a large north Pacific island to which he gave his name. Seventeen years earlier, Bruno Heceta, a Spaniard, had noted that currents and eddies between the two capes indicated that here was the mouth of a great river. He had not entered the stream, however. Now Captain Vancouver watched the surf breaking between the capes. He decided against chancing his vessel in such waters. Anyway, he concluded that no stream of consequence would be found inside the breakers.

So Vancouver coasted north for his meeting with the Spaniards, who, along with the Russians, laid claim to some of the seacoasts and uncharted interiors of this new country. While in the north, he explored and charted a large arm of the sea which he called Puget Sound for one of his officers.

While still sailing up the coast, he spoke a Yankee merchantman, the *Columbia* out of Boston, and exchanged information with Captain Robert Gray, its master. Captain Gray gave Captain Vancouver directions to the Strait of Juan de Fuca, which runs eastward from the Pacific to the sound. Vancouver, in turn, told Gray about his observations at the capes where Heceta's river was supposed to empty into the ocean.

A few days later, May 11, the *Columbia* stood off the capes. Captain Gray, unlike the British master, was convinced that here was the entrance to a river of considerable size. He decided to risk an entry and steered his ship east-northeast between the breakers. These soon subsided, and Gray found himself in a wide river. The water was fresh, clear out to the bar that he had just crossed, and his crew began at once to fill the ship's casks with it. Many canoes came alongside from an Indian village on the north side of the river. In exchange for a few nails, some cloth and a sheet of copper, the ship's company obtained many salmon and a considerable number of beaver and otter furs.

Captain Gray went ashore and took possession of the country in the name of the United States. But, whereas Captain Vancouver honored associates and important officials and noblemen in naming geographic points, the American skipper honored his ship. The great stream he discovered has been known ever since as the Columbia.

The crew of the *Columbia* did a little exploring but did not proceed far above the mouth. On May 20, Captain Gray sailed out over the bar and headed north for Nootka.

There he again met Captain Vancouver and with considerable satisfaction told about his discovery of the Great River of the West. The chagrined Vancouver determined that he too would enter the river, but when he arrived there in the fall the tumultuous waves on the bar drove him off. Lieutenant W. R. Broughton got through, however, with the tender

Chatham. In a longboat he was rowed ninety miles up the river where he named a snowy mountain for a nobleman, Admiral Samuel Hood, and took possession of the river and the land it drained in behalf of King George.

And so, within a period of a few months, a region, whose sole value up to then had appeared to be in its sea otter furs, was claimed by two not very friendly nations. Russia and Spain, the other contenders, eventually withdrew, the first to Alaska, the other to California.

Between the discovery voyages of Gray and Vancouver and the appearance of this book's first protagonist, both the United States and Great Britain had sought to strengthen their claims on the great northwest wilderness.

On the American side, the journey of Meriwether Lewis, former secretary to President Thomas Jefferson, and Captain William Clark, U.S.A., was the outstanding effort. The story of this expedition, in 1804–6, is familiar to everyone. The Lewis and Clark crossing of the northern Rockies was extremely difficult, though friendly Indians, especially Sacajawea, their woman guide, made it somewhat less so.

Lewis and Clark kindled a desire in Americans to extend their nation from the Atlantic to the Pacific. Their journal inspired further exploration that resulted in the discovery of an easier more-southern pass through the great mountain barrier. We shall see how this later breakthrough affected the settlement of the Northwest and determined that the Stars and Stripes, rather than the Maple Leaf emblem of Canada, should fly over it.

Another major American attempt to obtain control over the region was the establishment of Astoria at the mouth of the Columbia by men in the employ of John Jacob Astor, a German-born, wealthy merchant of New York. This was the first American settlement on the Pacific Coast. Astor sent one group by sea and another overland with orders to establish a fur trading post. Both parties suffered severe hardships and several members died. But in 1811, Astoria was established. In 1813, however, under threat of attack by a British warship which was expected momentarily, the partner in charge on the Columbia sold out to the North West Company. This Canadian organization changed the name of the place to Fort George.

It was this company that pushed forward for the British in the early years. In 1793, Alexander Mackenzie, a North West partner, brought a group of Canadian trappers over the Rockies into what is now British Columbia. In the years that followed, the company built posts in several parts of the Northwest. Besides Astoria at the Columbia's mouth, it had centers in the interior near present Spokane, Washington, Libby, Montana, Hope, Idaho, and on the Clark's Fork River in Montana.

In contrast with the Americans, the Canadians were successful west of the Rockies. When the North West Company merged with the British Hudson's Bay Company, following a bloody war between the two, the British-Canadian hold on the country became even stronger.

Astoria was returned to American sovereignty at the end of the War of 1812. But the Canadians still owned the little outpost, which later was abandoned when Hudson's Bay selected a better site about one hundred miles up the Columbia. This became the famed Fort Vancouver.

The diplomats who negotiated the disposition of United States–British claims at the end of the war could not agree on a border west of the Rocky Mountains. In 1818 they signed an agreement providing for equal rights for both nations in that part of the Northwest south of the 49th parallel, the line which separated the United States and British America east of the mountains. This arrangement continued for nearly thirty years. Both countries had sound claims to the far corner by discovery and exploration. The British had the advantage of being in the fur trade within this no-man's-land.

But east of the American Rockies, fur trapping also was developing under management of men from Missouri. Pressure built up behind the mountains, as the American trappers pressed farther and farther up the beaver streams toward the continental divide. The demand was brisk for furs from which to make the beaver hats then in fashion and cloaks for wealthy men in Europe and the eastern United States.

Advocates of United States settlement of the Pacific Northwest made themselves heard in Congress and in the newspapers, but many others could see no advantage in extending the country so far. And always there stood the great barrier of the Rockies. Settlers, with women, children and wagons, could not follow the difficult trails of Lewis and Clark and the Astor party. The sea lane around the tip of South America was too long a line of communication between East and West Coasts of the United States. An easier passage must be found.

Thus the situation, as our story opens, was this: The United States had equal claim with the British to a vast area bordered on the south by Mexican California, on the west by the Pacific Ocean and on the north by British America. On the east, the Rockies, the great "Shining Mountains," appeared to be an impenetrable bar to any serious attempt by United States citizens to take advantage of their rights.

The following accounts show how some Americans helped breach the barrier, how others assisted in winning the country for the young republic, and how still others took part in developing it after it had been won. The stories of only a dozen men and women of the thousands who have participated in the making of the Pacific Northwest can be told here. Obviously, many others did as much as these to create a large, prosperous addition to the United States. But the men and women who appear here are representative of their periods of time and of their sections of the great Northwest. Each made a lasting contribution to his region and to his country.

1 · JEDEDIAH SMITH —
THE TRAILBLAZER

Jedediah Smith was twenty-three years old when he straggled into St. Louis in the spring of 1822 and answered an advertisement that General William H. Ashley had inserted in the newspapers. The notice advised that Ashley, who was lieutenant governor of Missouri, and Major Andrew Henry, an old-time fur trapper, were organizing an expedition to trap beaver in the Rocky Mountains near the headwaters of the Missouri River. Men interested in participating in the venture were urged to call on the general.

Jedediah must have stood out among the bearded frontiersmen who applied for a chance to risk their lives for a share in the wealth the mountain streams were expected to yield, for he was far different from most of them. His face was clean shaven, and besides his rifle and traps he carried a small library. His two most treasured books were the Bible and a copy of the Lewis and Clark journal. They guided his eyes upward, the one toward Heaven and the other to the summit of whatever mountain he happened to be near.

The Lewis and Clark book had drawn the lean six-footer to this jumping-off place for the dangerous and unknown West. He had an ambition to see the country that Meriwether Lewis and Captain William Clark had described and to explore it more thoroughly than they had. The Bible charted his course as a devout, clean-living "shouting Methodist"; the explorers' journal was his inspiration to adventure.

The lithe young man evidently had no trouble obtaining a berth in the expedition. Though he was new to the Rockies, he

had lived most of his life on the fringe of the wilderness, first
in New York State, then in Pennsylvania and later in Ohio. He
knew his way about in the forests and on the Indian trails. The
previous winter he had trapped in Illinois, earning fifty dollars
for the season's work.

Diah, as his family called him, signed on as a hunter. In
May, 1822, he set out with a keelboat for the upper Missouri
River. His assignment was to roam the country along the
stream, shooting such game as he could find to supplement
the limited fare the boatmen had brought with them. One
day the boat to which he was attached, the *Enterprise*, capsized.
Ten thousand dollars worth of supplies and trade goods was
lost. This delayed the journey, but it finally was resumed with
a new boat and provisions.

Indian villages dotted the banks of the Missouri, but there
was little apprehension shown by Major Henry, commander
of the expedition, until the boats neared the twin towns of the
Arikaras. These lay on the right bank of the Missouri near
the mouth of the Grand River in southern South Dakota. The
Arikara houses were built of mud, grass, poles and crudely
fashioned timbers, and stood near a field in which corn was
grown. The disposition of the tribe was sometimes as ugly as
its lodges, and so Major Henry approached cautiously. If the
Rees, as they were generally called, were not hostile this time,
he would stop there and buy horses. The expedition needed
riding and pack animals when it penetrated the unnavigable
mountain streams near the continental divide.

Fortunately the Rees were friendly. The horses were
bought with trade goods, and the transaction was celebrated
by the smoking of the peace pipe and the eating of roasted
dog. Then the Americans got moving again, many of them
now mounted. Jedediah was dispatched with some of the others
to the mouth of the Musselshell River, where he spent the

winter.

Next spring, the now fairly seasoned mountain man was sent down the Missouri to meet General Ashley, who was coming upstream with two new keelboats, the *Yellow Stone Packet* and the *Rocky Mountains*. Jedediah was with the general when the boats hove into view of the Arikara villages. This time real trouble was expected with the unpredictable tribesmen. The report down river was that they were in a vicious mood.

However, General Ashley needed horses. He sent emissaries to Chiefs Little Soldier and Grey Eyes and told them he wished to buy forty animals. The chiefs were willing to trade. Ashley stipulated that the exchange of goods for horses should take place on a sand bar at the edge of the river, rather than in the villages. There was to be no fraternizing in the council lodge. The roast dog was passed up. A company of men, including Jedediah, was sent ashore to take charge of the purchases.

A few of the fur trappers, however, slipped into the villages to spend the night with the Indians. One of them, Aaron Stephens, was murdered. At daylight the men on the beach advanced toward the villages to demand Stephens' body and the murderer.

Suddenly the Rees began firing on the exposed shore party from the stockade of poles that surrounded the villages. Thunder and lightning, and rain in torrents, added to the confusion. The men on the boats, many of whom had been recruited in the river-front dives of St. Louis, were terror-stricken. They refused to go ashore to rescue the men on the beach.

Jedediah took command then. He and the others of the shore party returned the fire of the well-protected Indians until most of the trappers' horses were dead and many of the men dead or wounded. At last, the survivors had to take to the water.

Some of them drowned, but others, including Jedediah, made it to the boats which had been cut loose to drift out of range of the Rees. It was the most disastrous battle ever fought by the Missouri fur traders. Twelve men died in the battle and eleven were wounded, of whom two died later.

Jedediah Smith acquitted himself well. From that day forward he was regarded by the rough mountain men as a leader.

One of the wounded who later died was John Gardner. Before he succumbed he asked Hugh Glass, a mountain man, to write his family. Glass wrote these simple words:

My painful duty is to tell you of the death of yr Son wh befell at the hands of the Indians 2d of June in the early morning. He lived a little while after he was shot and asked me to inform you of his sad fate. We brought him to the ship, when he soon died.

Mr. Smith, a young man of our company, made a powerful prayer wh moved us all greatly, and I am persuaded John died in peace. His body we buried with others near this camp and marked the grave with a log.

Jedediah had found use not only for his rifle, but also for his Bible.

However, it was his skill with the rifle that won him his first command. This was of a small trapping party which left Fort Kiowa, downstream from the Arikara towns, in September, 1823. Fall was approaching, and if a proper wintering place was to be found in the distant Rockies, no more time could be lost. Therefore, Jedediah set his course straight west across the Badlands and the Black Hills of South Dakota.

Thomas ("Broken Hand") Fitzpatrick, a young Irishman of the same age as Smith, was second in command. William Sublette, also twenty-four, who would later become a partner of Jedediah and David E. Jackson in a famous fur-trapping company, was a member of the group. So was James Clyman, who kept a diary.

In the Black Hills, whose pines and junipers were a welcome relief from the dry Badlands, Jedediah met a grizzly bear and for the second time that year almost lost his life.

The little straggling column of men and horses was pushing its way late one afternoon through a narrow, brushy canyon. The horses were weak from the hard journey and the men were on foot, leading them. The yellow-brown grizzly, weighing probably a thousand pounds, came down a slope of the ravine and encountered the line of men and horses at about its middle. The bear turned and ran parallel to the column.

One can imagine the turmoil its appearance caused. The horses reared and neighed shrilly; the men shouted. Jedediah, who was at the head of the line, ran to open ground where the canyon widened to get a better aim at the intruder. As he emerged from the brush he met the bear head-on.

The great beast reared and sprang at the trapper's head. The young captain went sprawling, blood gushing from deep wounds on his head and face. The grizzly then clawed at the prostrate man's body, breaking several ribs. Worse injuries were prevented by the leather ball and powder pouches and the butcher knife Jedediah carried in his belt.

Who dispatched the bear, Jim Clyman does not say in his diary. Jedediah himself was in no position to do so. But shot it was. The great hide was sent down to St. Louis with the next shipment of beaver pelts, and one of the claws was preserved by the Smith family.

The mountain men, usually so competent in all manner of emergencies, did not know what to do with their wounded captain now. None of them had any surgical knowledge, and so they asked the barely conscious Jedediah himself for instructions.

"Send one or two men for water," the bloody leader told them. "Then if you have needle and thread, get them out and sew up my wounds."

Reluctantly, for he had little confidence in his ability as a surgeon, young Clyman produced scissors, as well as a needle and thread. Meanwhile he sent two men for water. He clipped the hair around the wounds and began to stitch up the gaping cuts on Jedediah's head and face.

"I found the bear had taken nearly all his head in his capacious mouth," wrote Clyman, "close to his left eye on one side and close to his right ear on the other, and laid the skull bare to near the crown of the head. . . ."

Clyman stitched the wounds as best he could until he came to the right ear, which was "torn from the head to the outer rim."

"I can't do anything for that ear," he told Smith.

"Oh, you must!" the injured man ordered. "Try to stitch it up someway or other."

So Clyman stitched it "through and through and over and over, laying the lacerated parts together as nice as I could."

Meanwhile the men who had gone for water returned. Jedediah's wounds were bathed, and he climbed on his horse and rode to camp, where two men and some of the weaker horses had been left.

After ten days in a tent, "Old Jed" was able to continue his journey westward, a couple of miles a day at first, then a few more. Trapping as it went, the little group of mountain men finally settled down for the winter with the Crow Indians on Wind River not far to the east of the continental divide.

Jedediah healed quickly in the cold mountain air. But his youthful handsomeness was gone forever. He had acquired a quizzical look, having now only one eyebrow, and he let his hair grow long to hide the mutilated ear.

Perhaps the young mountain man read a lot in the Lewis and Clark book that winter. By spring, in any event, he was extremely curious about what lay on the other side of the high mountains to the west of the camp. There ought to be beaver there, he reasoned. He asked some of the Crows if there was a passage between the towering peaks and ranges. They told him of a route they and other tribes often used.

Thus it was that on a bitterly cold March day in 1824 the tall scar-faced young man led his small band up a gradual but wind-swept slope near the Sweetwater River in what is now western Wyoming. By then, the men had been exposed for nearly a month to deep snow and gale-force winds. They were near exhaustion and their stomachs growled with hunger, because they had not eaten in four days. The wind which drove powder snow into their faces and covered their emaciated horses with ice also had driven nearly all the buffalo to warmer climates. Fortunately at least one of the shaggy beasts had remained behind. Two of the men found and shot it. Then they did not even try to build a fire. Instead they and the others, who soon came up, cut chunks of the warm, red meat from the carcass and gulped them down raw.

As the men struggled against the blizzard, they noticed that the slope now descended. They had crossed the continental divide. Jedediah made a mental note of the comparatively easy grade. Wagons could come this way, he thought. Someone at another time would designate this the South Pass, but the group of trappers had no time now to think of names. They had to get out of the frigid mountains and begin their search for beaver.

They felt their way down the ravines on the western side of the Rockies and presently came to the Green River in southwestern Wyoming and northeastern Utah. There they found many beaver, much game, good grass for their horses and pleasant shade among the willows on the river banks. In June, they took many peltries back across South Pass to rendezvous on the Sweetwater.

Jedediah was convinced that west of the Shining Mountains was a fur resource well worth exploiting. Exploit it he would, even beyond those other mountains on the far horizon. When the rendezvous had ended, he crossed the pass a third time, noting the plentiful supply of grass for horses and confirming his earlier conclusion that wagons could roll here with comparative ease.

Jedediah, with six other men, spent the late summer and fall of 1824 trapping and exploring hundreds of miles of the Pacific slope of the Rockies, where British Hudson's Bay Company "booshways" and their crews were already active. Jed was General Ashley's partner now, Major Henry having quit under stress of murderous and thieving attacks by the Blackfeet.

His first contact with the Hudson's Bay Company was made on the Snake River, near the present Blackfoot, Idaho, where the Americans ran across a band of Iroquois Indians who had come west to work for Hudson's Bay. The Iroquois had got into a fight with the Snake Indians and had been robbed of their horses, traps and virtually everything but the ragged clothes they wore and a cache of furs. They implored Jedediah to convoy them through hostile Indian country to Alexander Ross, the Hudson's Bay chief of this Snake River expedition. This Smith did in exchange for their beaver pelts. Ross reluctantly agreed to let the Americans join forces with him on the long trek to the British Flathead Post in northwestern Montana.

Ross considered Jedediah a spy, and he wasn't far wrong. The Hudson's Bay Company had for some months been concerned over the ever-nearing Americans. The order had gone out to trap the Snake River country bare of beaver to discourage the interlopers from the States. Now one of the most inquisitive of the invaders was on the company's own grounds. There was nothing wrong with Diah's eyes and he could still hear well with the torn ear, despite the long hair which concealed the scars, so he learned much about Hudson's Bay plans.

Jedediah explored as far as the Canadian border that winter. On the way back to the Ashley rendezvous on Henry's Fork of Green River, he got his first glimpse of the Great Salt Lake. Some say he was the first white man to see and wonder at this unusual body of water, but the honor probably belongs to Jim Bridger or Etienne Provost, who were there that same year.

However, Old Jed was a partner now with Ashley as supplier of the trappers, a promotion he had won by courage and leadership. He could not tarry by the lake. He had to get on to the rendezvous.

A mountain rendezvous was something to behold. From all directions came the white trappers, many accompanied by Indian wives. Great bands of Indians also came and pitched their camps all about. When all had gathered, the trader, in this case General Ashley, spread the supplies he had brought up from St. Louis. There were traps, guns and ammunition, of course, for these were the tools of the trade. But there were luxuries, too—coffee, tobacco, sugar and whisky for the men; ribbons, beads, scarlet cloth and bells for the women. The bells tinkled merrily when fastened to a squaw's saddle.

Pelts were bought by the trader at as low a price as possible and the goods sold to the white and Indian trappers for all the market would bear. Mountain men were always in debt.

But trading was only part of the pleasure to which the participants looked forward eagerly from one summer to the next. Carousing, gambling, horse racing, wrestling, foot racing and jumping made a rendezvous an uninhibited fair in the wilderness, with a cracked skull as a likely memento.

This rendezvous having ended finally, with no more than the usual casualties, Jedediah turned again to the west, this time intrigued by the deserts he had glimpsed near the Great Salt Lake.

Thus it happened that in late November, 1826, an Indian messenger galloped into Mission San Gabriel in far southern California with an urgent message for Father José Bernardo Sánchez. A day or two earlier, the messenger breathlessly informed Father Sánchez, a group of sixteen Americans had come riding across the San Bernardino Mountains to the green, well-watered valley over which the mission ruled. They had traversed the torrid desert lying west of the *Rio Colorado* and, in so doing, had exploded a myth. Mexican authorities, who then ruled California, had always believed the desert was an impenetrable barrier to invasion from the east. *El Capitan* Smith had proved it wasn't so.

Father Sánchez was a hospitable though startled man. When he had recovered his composure he gave orders to invite the strange *Yanquis* to the mission.

This first crossing from the Rockies to southern California had begun three months earlier at Bear Lake, which straddles the Idaho-Utah border. Jedediah, now a partner with David E. Jackson and William Sublette in a company that had just bought out General Ashley, was drawn to the Southwest by an unconquerable curiosity. He was his own boss now. He wanted to see how the land lay down there beyond the Great Salt Lake, picking up beaver pelts along the way, of course. So with a small company he struck out into the unknown.

So little was known of this *terra incognita* that some thought

Salt Lake was an arm of the sea, and others that a great river, called the Buenaventura, flowed from the valley of Salt Lake through the western mountains, emptying into the Pacific Ocean at San Francisco Bay. If such a river existed, it would be a splendid avenue by which to ship furs from the mountains. From the coast they could be reshipped to New York or the Orient.

Jedediah meant to find out if there was such a river. If it did exist, he might follow it to the sea, then go up the coast to the Columbia and back again to the next rendezvous at Bear Lake by way of the Columbia and the Snake. Or he might return by the Multnomah which Lewis and Clark believed paralleled the Snake far to the south and east before turning north through western Oregon.

Diah found no Buenaventura, of course. This river, the Sacramento, rises on the far side of the high Sierra Nevada, hundreds of miles to the west. He found no Multnomah (now called Willamette) either.

Jedediah and his companions did find a few small streams, but mostly they encountered great stretches of desert, in which many of their horses dropped dead one after the other, and in which lived a few impoverished Indians who existed on roots and crawling things.

After much exertion, they reached the Colorado River and a grassy valley where the Mojave Indians lived. There they rested for fifteen days, recuperating and trading their worn-out horses for fresh ones. Two men who had run away from a mission in California offered to guide them to that fabled land. And so the Americans struck off westward across the Mojave Desert, traveling some days from morning until night without water. At times they had to bury themselves in the sand to protect their bodies from the unmerciful sun.

For fifteen days the Americans endured these hardships.

Then they reached the summit of the San Bernardino Mountains and saw before them a broad valley, green with good grass and trees bordering a full-flowing stream.

Governor José Maria de Echeandia, enjoying the sun at San Diego, was not as hospitable as the kind padre at Mission San Gabriel. One can imagine his thoughts:

If these rude men are seeking furs in the Rocky Mountains, as their passport from General Clark in St. Louis permits them to do, what then are they doing way out here in California? This *capitan* has a strange look, especially when he raises his one eyebrow. Most likely he is a spy, and if he is allowed to go he will lead an army of *Americanos* back across the desert. This is something for Mexico City to pass upon.

For nearly two months Don José pondered the request of Captain Smith that he be permitted to buy horses and travel through California to San Francisco.

Finally, in early January, he said the Americans could go free. But they must return the way they came. They had seen enough of California already, probably more than was safe. But Jedediah decided that having come this far he was not to be swerved from his course, which lay straight north to the Columbia, more than one thousand miles away. Unknown to Don José, he led his group up through the interior valleys, camping finally on the American River, which got its name from his presence there.

The Americans had taken many beaver, but how were the pelts to be moved across the high mountains and deserts to the rendezvous on Bear Lake in far-off Idaho? Jedediah made an attempt to take his group across the Sierra, but had to turn back. He must leave most of his men and horses, he decided, along with the furs, in camp on Stanislaus River. He and two others, Silas Gobel and Robert Evans, would make their way barehanded to the rendezvous. He would be back in four months, Jedediah told Harrison Rogers, his clerk, who took charge on the Stanislaus.

On May 20, Jedediah and his two companions started up the north fork of the Stanislaus on the first crossing of the Sierra Nevada ever made by white men. They had seven horses and two mules, carrying hay for the animals and food for the men. In eight days they crossed the mountains, losing two horses and one mule on the precipices. After the mountains, came six hundred miles of barren wasteland. Here was no game. A few Indians were seen who lived on grass seed and grasshoppers. Smith, Gobel and Evans ate three of the horses as they gave out. The remaining animals could hardly carry the few supplies left. The men almost died of thirst. But they made it to the rendezvous.

"My arrival caused a considerable bustle in camp," concludes Jedediah's account of this harrowing journey, "for myself and party had been given up as lost. A small Cannon brought up from St. Louis was loaded and fired for a salute."

Now he faced the task of rejoining the men he had left in California. Mid-August, 1827, found Jedediah and eighteen men again among the Mojaves on the Colorado. He didn't know that between his visits to the Mojaves, the Indians had lost several men in a battle with a group of white men under Ewing Young, trapping out of New Mexico. This time, Jedediah remained with the Mojaves only three days, trading congenially enough for beans, dried pumpkins, corn and wheat. Then he started to cross the Colorado on reed rafts as he had done a year earlier.

Half of the Americans remained with the horses on the left bank while the captain and the rest of the company embarked with the firearms and merchandise on the frail craft. No sooner had the rafts reached midstream than the Mojaves attacked the unarmed Americans left behind. Evidently the redmen had been waiting for an opportunity to even the score with the whites. Ten men died on the hostile shore. Jedediah and the eight men still living shouldered the few supplies they could carry and began the long hike on foot across the desert toward California.

"Old Jed's" knowledge of the Mojave Desert from the previous year made the long walk across it possible. He knew where water was to be found. He managed also to obtain from a band of Indians a few horses by trading knives, beads and cloth the men had in the packs. The group reached the San Bernardino Valley in late August and camped there five days. They reached the camp on the Stanislaus on September 18, two days before expiration of the four months Jedediah had given himself for his round trip to the rendezvous.

"I was there by the time appointed but instead of Bringing them the expected supplies I brought them intelligence of my misfortune," wrote Jedediah.

To obtain the necessary supplies Smith decided to travel to Mission San José. There the welcome was the opposite of that received the year before at Mission San Gabriel. The reverend fathers showed Jedediah to the guardhouse and kept him there two days. Finally, through the intervention of William Welch, an American living at Pueblo San José; Captain John Rogers Cooper, a Bostonian living at Monterey; and Thomas B. Park, supercargo on the brig *Harbinger* from Boston, Jedediah was taken to Monterey to see the governor, the same Don José he had dealt with at San Diego the previous winter.

Weeks passed while the uncertain Don José considered the case, and for a short time Jedediah was locked up in prison at Monterey. At mid-November, the governor gave the American a passport. Captain Cooper by bond guaranteed his good conduct. The furs from the cache on the Stanislaus were traded for horses and equipment, and on December 30 Jedediah and his party set out for the north.

The trapper-explorer now had an opportunity to trace the Sacramento, the "Buenaventura" that earlier men had believed flowed from the Rockies to the sea.

Besides his men, he had 250 horses and mules. The animals he had bought at ten dollars each in exchange for his furs. He thought that since he had few pelts to bring back to next year's rendezvous he would bring mounts and pack animals to sell at a profit.

His course was up the Sacramento, then across the Coast Range to the ocean, up the coast and inland again to the Willamette and thence to the Columbia. The group crossed the Sacramento just above Red Bluff on April 11 and began working its way to a pass Diah could see in the western mountains. In this country, there were giant evergreens and plenty of water. But it was one of the roughest journeys Jedediah ever made.

For more than two months the party pushed slowly down the Hay Fork of the Trinity River and the Klamath River before it could travel with any degree of ease along the Oregon coast. Indians shot at them with arrows from the canyon rims, horses fell down the precipitous walls of the ravines. Fog obliterated the country, making it nearly impossible to pick out gaps through the mountains.

On July 13, 1828, a Sunday, the expedition camped on the Umpqua River in Oregon at its juncture with its north branch, which from that day to this would be known as Smith River. Indians of the area told them they could reach the Hudson's Bay post at Fort Vancouver if they went up the Umpqua to Elk River, then over the Calapooya Mountains to the Willamette.

However, there had been trouble with the Indians. On

Saturday, one of them had stolen an ax—the only one the trappers possessed. The white men seized him and tied a rope around his neck. They let him go only after he gave up the ax.

On Monday, Jedediah and two of his men, Richard Leland and John Turner, set out from camp in a canoe to find solid ground for a trail through the swampy country. A little later, contrary to orders Jedediah had given him, Rogers admitted about one hundred Indians to the camp. Unknown to Rogers, the Indians were bent on revenge for the indignity to the ax thief and also to one of the chiefs Arthur Black had ordered to dismount from a horse belonging to the Americans.

The trappers' weapons were wet from crossing the river, and while they were laying them out to dry, the men were rushed by the Indians. Arthur Black managed to escape and wandered up the coast. Eventually he fell in with friendly Tillamook Indians who guided him across the Coast Range to the Willamette.

On the night of August 8, Dr. John McLoughlin, factor of the Hudson's Bay Company, was aroused by a clamor at the gate of Fort Vancouver.

"We've brought an American!" Indians outside shouted.

Dr. McLoughlin ordered the gate opened and in stumbled the shadow of a man, who, after he had rested awhile, said he was Arthur Black, probably the only survivor of a party of eighteen Americans captained by Jedediah Smith.

Dr. McLoughlin organized a party of forty men to conduct a search for possible survivors. However, before this group could get under way, Smith, Leland and Turner arrived. They told of returning to the camp on the Umpqua to find it silent and all the Americans apparently dead. Like Black, they had gone up the coast to the Tillamook village, and these friendly Indians had guided them also to Fort Vancouver.

Dr. McLoughlin was a man of impressive stature. He stood over six feet, and a shock of long white hair added to his striking appearance. He was strong willed, and ruled his fur empire with a firm hand. But he had compassion and a sense of honor almost to a fault. He received Jedediah Smith and the other sorry survivors of the Umpqua massacre with the same openhandedness that missionaries and American settlers were to marvel at in later years.

Not only did McLoughlin take in these men who threatened the Hudson's Bay Company monopoly in the Oregon country; he ordered Alex McLeod and twenty-two *engagés* to accompany Jedediah and his three men back to the Umpqua to recover what they could of the American's furs, horses and equipment. At the mouth of Smith River they found the skeletons of eleven of Smith's men. Under prodding from McLeod, the Indians returned several hundred beaver pelts—trapped on the long journey over the Coast Mountains—along with some of the stolen horses and a few guns, cooking utensils and other items. In early December the party sadly returned to Fort Vancouver in a downpour, hampered by rain-swollen streams.

While Jedediah and McLeod were on the Umpqua, Governor George Simpson of York Factory on Hudson Bay arrived at Fort Vancouver. Simpson, who had little regard for the "adventurers" who engaged in the American fur trade but who nevertheless was concerned about their invasion of his terrain, sought to learn from Jedediah what the latter had discovered on his wide and disastrous travels through the West. Meanwhile he agreed to buy for $2,369.60 the furs and horses that had been recovered on the Umpqua.

One wonders if Jedediah told his story in the same way to Simpson as he was later to write it to American officials. Maybe wishful thinking influenced Simpson's understanding of its import.

Smith had revealed, the Hudson's Bay man wrote his London office, that there was much interest among Americans in the possibility of settling the Willamette Valley. American charts indicated that the Willamette River rose in the Rocky Mountains and some of the prospective settlers believed they could embark, with their horses, cattle and agricultural implements, on large rafts or bateaux and glide down the current 800 to 1000 miles at their ease to the "land of promise." But Smith's explorations, Simpson recounted, had proved this could not be done. The Willamette River rose not in the Rockies but only 150 miles from Fort Vancouver, in mountains that even hunters would not attempt to penetrate.

"I am of the opinion we have little to apprehend from Settlers in this quarter, and from Indian Traders nothing," concluded Simpson. "I feel perfectly at ease unless the all grasping policy of the American Government should induce it to embark some of its National Wealth in furtherance of this object."

Jedediah stayed at Vancouver until spring. That summer he was reunited with his partners, David Jackson and William Sublette, at Pierre's Hole by the Tetons. Jackson and Sublette had given Jedediah up for lost and rejoiced to see him alive and hearty. But they decided this would be their last year in the mountains. Though barely past their twenties, they were too old for trapping.

Significantly this last year was to bring the first wagon trains over the plains clear to the Rockies. William Sublette brought ten 1800-pound freight wagons from St. Louis to the rendezvous at Wind River. This first of the wagon trains presaged one of history's most spectacular migrations.

Smith, Jackson and Sublette sold their business to five other mountain men at the close of the rendezvous, and Jedediah rode with the wagons back to St. Louis. There he wrote a letter to Secretary of War John H. Eaton which was printed in a Senate document and reprinted by newspapers in many parts of the country. Its implications were just the reverse of what George Simpson had inferred from his talks with Jedediah at Fort Vancouver. It was to help give rise to the "Oregon fever," which carried Americans by the thousands over South Pass, along the Snake and down the Columbia.

In the letter, written in the name of all three partners, an account was given of the driving of the wagons to the Rockies:

This is the first time that wagons ever went to the Rocky Mountains, and the ease and safety with which it was done prove the facility of communicating over land with the Pacific Ocean. The route from the *Southern Pass,* where the wagons stopped, to the Great Falls of the Columbia, being easier and better than on this side of the mountains, with grass enough for horses and mules, but a scarcity of game for the support of men.

The letter described the activities of the Hudson's Bay Company which Jedediah had observed during his stay at Fort Vancouver. It told of the improvements made there, of the sawmill and gristmill in operation, of the presence of cannon, of the building of two coasting vessels, one of which had been on a voyage to the Sandwich Islands (Hawaii), and of fields of grain and other crops. "So that every thing seemed to combine to prove that this fort was to be a permanent establishment."

The letter concluded:

As to the injury which must happen to the United States from the British getting the control of all the Indians beyond the mountains, building and repairing ships in the tide water region of the Columbia, and having a station there for their privateers and vessels of war, is too obvious to need a recapitulation. . . .

Jedediah didn't live to see the hundreds of prairie schooners flowing through South Pass and on to the green meadows of the "Wilhamot." He never knew that the Pacific Northwest was saved for the United States in large measure due to his own brave exploits.

The tattered-eared trapper who had been the first American to see so much of the western wilderness was uncomfortable among the comforts of St. Louis. In 1831 he set out for Santa Fe with a wagon train of merchandise, a routine mission. But Jedediah's luck ran out. Scouting ahead for water, as he had always done, he ran into a band of Comanches, and he died on the Cimarron by the Santa Fe Trail with a lance through his body. "Old Jed" was thirty-three.

2 · NARCISSA WHITMAN—
BLOND MARTYR OF WAIILATPU

The scene again is South Pass. The time is July 4, 1836. On the ridgepole of the continent sits a statuesque, golden-haired woman on a horse. She turns in her sidesaddle as she sweeps the western horizon with her shaded eyes.

Narcissa Whitman, bride of less than five months, is looking toward "heathen lands." For a dozen years she has yearned to save savage souls.

It is another momentous day in the wide gap through the Rockies where Jedediah Smith foresaw a stream of immigrants. So far there had been only a trickle, but the flood is building up back east beyond the Missouri. The comely, blond woman and a darker, less magnetic one, Eliza Hart Spalding, who is resting in a light wagon with yellow wheels, are the first of their sex and race to come this far and go on across the Rockies.

One may be sure that Narcissa looks back over the road she has come, as well as forward into the unknown. She has been looking back often to home in Steuben County, New York, in recent weeks on the plain. From the divide onward, her memories will become increasingly poignant. The fly-blown, dried buffalo meat they have bought from the Indians will turn bitter in her mouth as she thinks of the bread Mother used to bake and of pork and potatoes. While they rest she will talk with her husband, of the Prentiss house in Angelica, of the large, happy family there, of the Presbyterian Church where she sang with a voice as golden as her hair.

But enough of reverie for now. Here come the Nez Perce

chiefs to bid them welcome. She must dismount to shake their hands, as Dr. Whitman, the Reverend Henry Spalding and William Gray are doing. Tonight the men will discuss the future with Chiefs Lawyer and Rottenbelly.

Narcissa Prentiss decided to become a missionary at age sixteen. Years later, when she made formal application to the American Board of Commissioners for Foreign Missions, she remembered the exact day when she consecrated herself to work among the heathen. It was the first Monday in January, 1824.

To understand why a pretty teen-age girl, whose heart was as light as her hair, should dedicate herself to a drab existence among savages, one must consider the time. During the early half of the nineteenth century, the nation was swept by a wave of religious revivalism. The command of the Saviour, "Go ye therefore, and teach all nations," was as real to hundreds of young men and women as it had been to the disciples on the mountain in Galilee eighteen centuries earlier. There was a tinge of romanticism and love of adventure, too, in Narcissa's sincere desire to serve.

Thus it was not entirely unnatural that the blond, buoyant daughter of "Judge" Stephen Prentiss should wish to give up her happy life in western New York. But opportunities for young women to spread the gospel in pagan lands were not plentiful. Narcissa had to put aside her desire and content herself with teaching the children of Prattsburg and Angelica. To do this she obtained an education unusually good for the time.

As daughter of one of the county's leading citizens and as the oldest and loveliest of the five Prentiss girls, Narcissa did not walk home unescorted from services and choir practice at the Presbyterian Church. There were many suitors in the large Prentiss parlor. One of them was Henry Harmon Spalding, a student for the ministry who also had a deep desire to be a missionary. Narcissa rejected him, along with the others, and he never forgave her.

As the years passed and Narcissa approached the age when young women were considered old maids, her hope to serve the Lord in foreign fields must have faded. There is no evidence, however, that she became morose. Her lighthearted nature didn't change. She enjoyed the happy family circle and praised the Lord in song.

Then, in 1831, came a new challenge for missionaries. In that year four Nez Perce and Flathead Indians from the Northwest accompanied a fur brigade to St. Louis. The Indians, impressed by the white men's "medicine," had come to plead for the Book and the "black gowns" which seemed to be an important component of the whites' superior power.

An account of the visit appeared in the *Christian Advocate*, and several Protestant missionary leaders were stirred to answer the call ahead of the "black gowns," which was an obvious reference to Catholic priests. Methodist Jason Lee was the first to cross the Rockies into the Pacific Northwest, which now suddenly appeared more important than older fields on other continents. In 1834, he led a small group across South Pass. But he didn't stop in Nez Perce or Flathead country. He continued to the Willamette Valley in what is now western Oregon and established his mission near present-day Salem.

Another group aroused by the emotional article in the *Advocate* was the American Board of Commissioners for Foreign Missions, an organization jointly sponsored by Presbyterian, Congregational and Dutch Reformed churches. The board sent middle-aged Dr. Samuel Parker west in 1834, but he arrived too late to cross the divide. He returned home to Ithaca, New York, to raise funds and enlist assistants for another journey the following year.

Dr. Parker drove about western New York that winter, speaking in the churches of the need for missionaries and money to save the heathen Indians of the Northwest. Dr. Marcus Whitman, thirty-two-year-old country doctor, offered to go to the Oregon Country as a medical missionary, and Parker urged him to apply to the board for the assignment.

At Angelica, Narcissa Prentiss heard Dr. Parker's plea, and her dim but never forgotten hope to become a missionary was reawakened. After the meeting had closed with a hymn, in which her golden voice rang with more than usual emotion, Narcissa asked the visitor if the board would consider an unmarried woman for missionary work. He promised to find out.

Dr. Whitman's application was approved by the board and he called on Dr. Parker at Ithaca to obtain further instructions. Parker happened to think of Narcissa Prentiss. She might make a splendid wife and helper for the medical practitioner in the wilderness, the older man thought. Whitman evidently was intrigued by Parker's description of the beautiful, devout young woman. Soon he was off to Angelica to call on her.

So it happened that in one short week end Narcissa became engaged to be married and also achieved the religious goal to which she had so long aspired. She must have been a happy young woman indeed when the tall, husky Marcus took his leave at the Prentiss front door.

He had explained, though, that the marriage would have to be delayed for a year or so. He and Dr. Parker must go west to scout the country before he took his bride there. This they did in the summer of 1835. Dr. Parker went on to the Pacific, but Whitman returned from the Rockies to find a minister of the gospel for the missionary team, to raise necessary funds and, of course, to marry. He enlisted Henry Spalding, now a minister, and Eliza Hart Spalding, Henry's wife, to go with him and Narcissa to Oregon. It is not clear whether Marcus then knew that Spalding had once been Narcissa's suitor and that the thin, stooped clergyman still deeply resented her rejection of him.

When Marcus had completed these arrangements, he hurried to Angelica. There on the third Thursday of February, 1836, the blond, shapely schoolteacher, now twenty-eight years old, and the rugged, sandy-haired physician were married.

Narcissa had chosen a black bombazine wedding dress, not because the thought of marriage depressed her, but because such a dress could be worn for many years in the wilderness. There is in fact indication that the bride was jubilant. The Reverend Mr. Leverett Hull of the Angelica Presbyterian Church had chosen as the closing hymn, "Yes, My Native Land, I Love Thee!":

> Yes, my native land! I love thee;
> All thy scenes I love thee well;
> Friends, connections, happy country,
> Can I bid you all farewell?
> Can I leave you,
> Far in heathen lands to dwell?

There was no doubt in Narcissa's voice. The congregation broke down with emotion, but the stately, blond bride sang on to the end, her soprano voice clear and jubilant.

Marcus and Narcissa Whitman hastened by sleigh, wagons, steamboats and horses westward toward the heathen land and martyrdom. The trail before them held many dangers. Sometimes death was instant in a swollen stream, on a precipitous mountain or from the musket ball or arrow of a hostile Indian. At other times it was lingering, from cholera or dysentery. The weapons against death that Marcus Whitman, M.D., carried in his saddlebags were ineffective, indeed, in that day when calomel was the country doctor's "wonder drug." But the doctor and his wife were not entirely dependent on drugs; their faith was strong.

Narcissa hardly knew the husky six-footer whose life as a missionary she had sworn to share. Their courtship had been a strange one. But now they had a brief time to form the warm relationship of man and wife as they traveled east to Ithaca, west to Rushville where Marcus's family lived, by sleigh to Pittsburgh and by steamer down the Ohio River to Cincinnati.

Narcissa soon grew to love the practical, often stubborn man, five years her senior, whom she was always to refer to adoringly as "Husband." In an early letter home, she confided in her mother:

"I think I should like to whisper . . . many things which I cannot write. If only I could see you in your room for one-half hour. This much I can [say], mother. I have one of the kindest of husbands, and the very best in every way. . . ."

Beyond Cincinnati, where the Henry Spaldings waited, there was scant opportunity for honeymooning. The two couples were thrown together constantly, on the steamers and in the towns where they always rested on the Sabbath. In St. Louis and later at Liberty, near the present Kansas City, there were supplies to be bought and much preparation to make for the long, hard ride across the plains and mountains.

Narcissa took a liking to Eliza at once. The women were opposites, one buxomly attractive and ebullient, the other plain, frail and quiet. Their husbands formed as much of a contrast. Marcus was strong and husky; the Reverend Mr. Spalding was lean and rawboned with stooping shoulders and thinning dark hair. He had a contentious spirit as well. Narcissa must often have felt uncomfortable under the cold, critical eyes of her former suitor who openly asserted that she was a woman of poor judgment.

At Liberty the missionaries were joined by William H. Gray, who had been assigned to them by the board as a lay assistant. There Whitman and Spalding acquired a heavy wagon, twelve horses, six mules and seventeen head of cattle. The big wagon was their second vehicle. The other, a light Deerborn which Spalding had brought from New York State, was to go all the way to the Snake River, its yellow wheels making the first ruts in the Oregon Trail west of the Rockies.

The journey across the plains was a delight to the eager Narcissa, who had never been far from home. She enjoyed fording the streams, riding on the tallest horses to keep her skirts dry. When she saw her first buffalo, she persuaded the ailing Eliza to run up a hill with her to get a better view of the shaggy herd. She wrote home with great enthusiasm about all this, remembering always the family and sharing with them the excitement of the trail.

She found it exhilarating to be awakened at the break of day by "Arise! Arise!" shouted by members of the fur brigade, in whose dust the missionaries traveled day after day. The three-hour breaks at noon she described as a schoolgirl might tell of a picnic. She related:

Our table is the ground. Our table cloth is an India rubber cloth. . . . Our dishes are made of tin, tin basin for tea cups, iron spoons and plates. . . . Each one carries his own knife in his scabbard. . . . Husband always provides my seat and in a way that you would laugh to see us. . . . We take a blanket and lay down by the table. . . .

The "lady" even had a tea party. Her guests were Thomas ("Broken Hand") Fitzpatrick, leader of the fur brigade, and several "gentlemen of the Company who are going over the Mountains for pleasure"—Captain Stewart, Major Harris and Mr. Celam. She brewed the tea on a fire of buffalo chips, which she described as somewhat similar to Pennsylvania coal.

Fitzpatrick had not been very polite to the missionaries. He was in a hurry to reach the rendezvous at Green River. He refused to wait for them, and they were always hurrying to catch up to his train of four hundred animals, seventy men, seven large wagons and a cart. Nevertheless, he succumbed to Narcissa's charm. And there he was, having tea on a Monday evening with a missionary's lady and some blooming Englishmen. Old Broken Hand probably was gruffer than usual next day with his crew, lest they think him soft.

The mountain men and many bands of Indians had been waiting impatiently at the rendezvous for a week. Then a messenger arrived from Fitzpatrick with exciting news. The caravan would be along in a few days, the courier said, and there were two white women with it!

Joe Meek and half a dozen fellow trappers decided to welcome the unusual guests in true mountain fashion. First they made themselves presentable. Some even shaved, for the first time in months. Everyone saw to it that his buckskin breeches were decent. Many of the mountain men hadn't seen a white woman for years; most of the Indians had never seen one. Their preparations completed, the trappers and several Indians leaped on their horses and rode off toward South Pass.

Perhaps Narcissa was a little frightened, when over the brow of a hill the welcoming party came galloping, whooping and hollering and shooting their guns in the air. But more likely she was delighted. In the next few days, as she and Eliza rested in their tent of bed ticking in the shade of the willows by Green River, she was the center of an admiring throng of near-savage white men. The men were extraordinarily courteous in the presence of white ladies, who reminded them of mothers, sisters and sweethearts.

Some of the mountain men spent hours talking with Narcissa and Eliza. The more bashful ones walked by, touching their fur caps when the golden-haired beauty and the dark, quiet lady took notice of them. Narcissa may have sung to the men in her mellow soprano—hymns, of course. But the Indians were drawn more to Eliza than to her livelier companion, perhaps sensing a deeper dedication to their welfare. Both had been touched by the warm welcome of the Nez Perce women.

Fitzpatrick turned back at Green River. John McLeod and Thomas McKay of the Hudson's Bay Company guided the missionaries on the remaining shorter but more difficult part of the journey to the Columbia.

After crossing the divide, the quiet, capable, dedicated Eliza became stronger, now that her goal was near. Narcissa's journal shows that she, on the other hand, became daily more tired and homesick. She realized at last that bonds with home and family had been severed probably forever.

The fading Narcissa wrote:

Yesterday the 22nd [July] was a tedious day to us. . . . I thought of Mother's bread & butter many times as any hungry child would, but did not find it on the way. I fancy pork & potatoes would relish extremely well. Have been living on fresh meat for two months exclusively. Am cloyed with it. I do not know how I shall endure this part of the journey. . . .

A few days later:

Very mountainous. . . . Passed a creek on which were a fine bunch of gooseberries, nearly ripe. Relished them very much. . . . Husband had a tedious time with the waggon today. Got set in the creek this morning while crossing, was obliged to wade considerably in getting it out. After that in going between two mountains . . . the waggon was upset twice. Did not wonder at this at all. It was a greater wonder that it was not turning a somerset continually. It is not very greatful to my feelings to see him wear out with such excessive fatigue. . . .

By July 27, Narcissa no longer was cloyed with fresh meat:

We have plenty of dry buffalo meat which we purchased of the Indians & dry it is for me. I can scarcely eat it, it appears so filthy, but it will keep us alive & we should be thankful for it. . . . Found no berries. Neither have I found any of Ma's bread. (Girls do not waste the bread. If you know how well I should relish even the dryest morsel you would save every piece carefully.)

Then, perhaps to bolster her own spirits as much as to reassure the family back in Angelica, she added: "Do not think I regret coming. No, far from it. I would not go back for a world. I am contented & happy notwithstanding I get very hungry & weary. . . ."

It would be unfair to infer that Narcissa had only thoughts for her own comfort. Her reaction to the trials of the hard journey was influenced in no small degree by the fact that she was by now an expectant mother. Despite her own discomfort, she was solicitous of her fellow travelers. She pitied the Indian women who, she remarked, traveled like this all their lives and knew no ease. They were the "complete slaves" of their husbands, doing all the work, such as getting the wood, preparing the food, pitching their lodges, and packing and driving the animals.

"I am making a little progress in their language," noted Narcissa. "I long to converse with them about the Saviour. They all appear anxious to converse with us and to be understood by us."

Unfortunately, Narcissa was never fully to understand them, nor they her.

The men of the Hudson's Bay Company did their best to make the journey as easy as possible. McLeod was kind to the handsome woman from New York. He shared his game with her and often invited the Americans to tea. Sometimes, when the missionaries were slow in reaching camp at night, Narcissa found her tent already pitched.

Narcissa was a bit put out about Husband's and Spalding's insistence on taking the light wagon with them to their destination. Narcissa wrote on July 28:

One of the axle trees of the waggon broke today. Was a little rejoiced, for we were in hopes that they would leave it & have no more trouble with it. Our rejoycing was in vain, however, for they are making a cart of the hind wheels this afternoon & lashing the forward wheels to it, intending to take it through in some shape or other. They are so resolute & untiring in their efforts they will probably succeed.

Marcus and Henry had to give in finally. They left the cart and extra wheels at Fort Boise. Narcissa relished the short stays under roofs at Fort Hall, near present Pocatello, Idaho, and at Boise. But beyond the Snake the heat and long rides through the sagebrush sapped both her energy and her spirit. Then, near the end of the journey, she revived again.

The Blue Mountains made Narcissa think of the hills in her native county Steuben. Riding through the pleasant forests, she frequently met old acquaintances, in the trees & flowers & was not a little delighted. Indeed I do not know as I was ever so much affected with any scenery in my life. The singing of the birds, the echo of the voices of my fellow travelers, as they scattered through the woods, all had a strong resemblance to bygone days.

From the summit she saw for the first time her new home. The broad valley of the Columbia was spread out before her. In the far distance she could see snow-covered Mount Hood and Mount St. Helens. The sun was just sinking behind the western horizon as the travelers reached the summit and started to descend and the peaks were silhouetted against the pink sky. The beauty of the scene and the tranquility of the twilight, which contrasted so strongly with the rough country of the past several weeks, enchanted the tired woman. She quite forgot for a time how weary she really was.

It was a short journey now to Fort Nez Perce (Walla Walla), the Hudson's Bay post on the Columbia, thirty miles from the present city of Walla Walla, Washington. There the missionaries were welcomed warmly by Chief Trader Pierre Chrysologue Pambrun and his Cree Indian wife. One can almost hear Narcissa's sigh of contentment as she sank into a cushioned arm chair; the saddle she had sat on so many weeks was far from soft.

The Pambruns set a bountiful table. There were even pork and potatoes and bread and butter! A "mushmellon" nineteen inches in diameter was the finest Narcissa had ever eaten!

The Whitmans and Spaldings, however, did not tarry at Fort Nez Perce. They must be off down river to Fort Vancouver to buy supplies. Yet compared with the hard ride across the plains and mountains, the boat trip down the Columbia was a delight. It introduced Narcissa to a pleasant interlude.

The gently bred woman felt as if she had returned to civilization when she saw the buildings of the Hudson's Bay Company. "The New York of the Pacific Ocean" was the way she described the establishment of kindly Dr. John McLoughlin. Two ships were lying in the harbor, one of which had just arrived from London.

Narcissa charmed the people of Vancouver. Mrs. McLoughlin, daughter of a Swiss-Canadian merchant and an Indian woman, became her favorite companion. They took long rides together, Mrs. McLoughlin riding astride the horse, as her mother had done, and the proper lady from the East clinging to her sidesaddle.

The small-town woman from Angelica marveled at the cosmopolitan life. Each course at table was served on a fresh plate! There was wine on the tables—though the missionaries did not drink it—and the "gentlemen frequently drink toasts to each other."

Narcissa tutored Eloisa Maria, the McLoughlins' daughter. Nearly every evening she sang with the children of the French Canadian trappers and their Indian wives.

Meanwhile, the men laid their plans for the future. It is significant that the difficult Spalding and the often-stubborn Whitman decided on two missions rather than a joint one. Dr. Whitman chose to settle with the Cayuse tribe at Waiilatpu, "The Place of the Rye Grass," six miles from the present city of Walla Walla. The Reverend Mr. Spalding decided on a place among the Nez Perce at Lapwai, near present Lewiston, Idaho. The men left Vancouver for upriver in late September.

Dr. McLoughlin urged Narcissa and Eliza to stay all winter. Narcissa's baby was expected in the spring, and the kindly factor thought she would be better cared for at Vancouver. But the women wished to be with their husbands, and on

November 3 they left by bateaux on an eighteen-day voyage up the Columbia.

Early in December Marcus took his wife to a leanto, a crude building of roughly sawed timbers chinked with mud. But it had a cheerful fireplace, and Narcissa congratulated herself that it was a much better place than poor Eliza would live in over winter. The Spaldings had only a lodge of animal skins.

Narcissa tried hard to make friends with the Indians, leading the children in singing, teaching them to read and participating in the religious services. But they frightened her by staring through the windows and walking through the house at will.

"The Old Chief Umtippe has been a savage creature in his day," she wrote home. "His heart is still the same, full of all manner of hypocracy, deceit and guile. He is a mortal beggar as all Indians are. . . ."

Little Alice Clarissa, born March 14, on the eve of Narcissa's own birthday, provided many joyful hours, but she was doomed to tragedy. When a little past two, the child toddled down to the river and drowned. It happened on a Sabbath when the Whitmans, as usual, were resting.

In May, many of the Indians took sick with a lung inflammation. Dr. Whitman cared for them, but often they failed to follow his instructions. When they suffered relapses they called in their *tewat* doctors. The Indian medicine men were invariably held personally responsible when their patients died.

"Umtippe got into a rage about his wife," reported Narcissa, "& told my Husband while she was under his care that if his wife died that night he should kill him."

In late summer, 1838, nine persons came across the plains to help Whitman and Spalding. Instead of helping, they caused trouble. Tensions grew among the missioners crowded together for the winter at Waiilatpu. Voices often were louder in dispute than in prayer.

"We have a strange company of missionaries," wrote Mrs. Elkanah Walker, one of the newcomers. "Scarcely one who is not intolerable on some account."

"I was nearly exhausted," wrote Narcissa, "both in body and mind, in the labor and care of our numerous family." The tired mistress of Waiilatpu became subject to spells of despondency. She shut herself in her room and wept.

After much argument, the Cushing Eells and the Walkers went to a new mission, Tshimakain, thirty miles from the present city of Spokane. The others remained at Waiilatpu and Lapwai.

Causing additional concern for Whitman was the arrival of the first "black gowns"—Catholic missionaries Francois Norbert Blanchet and Modeste Demers, who energetically preached to Indians and others all over the Northwest. The presence of the priests aroused in Marcus a new conception of his duties in Oregon. Worry lest the United States lose Oregon began to interfere with his efforts to save the souls of the Indians. In his mind the Protestants represented the United States. The Catholics, on the other hand, were connected with the Hudson's Bay and, therefore, represented the British.

In October, 1842, Whitman set out for the East, riding for weeks through deep snow and hostile Indian country. But the hazardous journey was not made to "save Oregon," as a later legend claimed, but to save his mission. The contentious missionaries had sent critical reports back to the board. In addition, Waiilatpu had become more of a tavern for travelers than the mission to the Indians the board intended it to be. So the board had sent orders to close Waiilatpu and Lapwai.

Whitman had to go east to plead for a reversal of the decision. He saved the missions, by earnest argument.

Marcus' departure left Narcissa at Waiilatpu with only three half-breed children, whom the Whitmans had taken in, and an Hawaiian boy who had been hired to work at the mission. The lonely woman was uneasy, for there had been serious trouble with the Indians before Marcus went away. On one occasion old Chief Tilaukait had struck the missionary with his fist. Another time, one of the chief's men had pulled the doctor's ear. When Marcus turned the other ear, the Indian pulled it as well. Whitman had been threatened also with rifle, ax and hammer by two of the Indians.

One night soon after Marcus left, Narcissa was awakened by the lifting of the latch on her door. An intruder forced his way into her room, and she struggled with him in the dark. Her screams sent her assailant fleeing. Obviously she and her wards were not safe alone at Waiilatpu. Archibald McKinlay, who had succeeded Pambrun at Fort Walla Walla, heard of the attack and sent a wagon to fetch her and the children to the fort. In late October, Narcissa went to The Dalles as guest of the Methodist missionaries.

The frightened, lonely, once-bouyant woman spent much time weeping. On her birthday, in March, she wrote to Julia and Augustus Whitman at Rushville, New York:

"Need I ask you how you enjoy the society of your dear brother. . . . His society was my life and while I had him I never knew that I was lonely. Now I am restless and uneasy, numbering the past, anxiously looking forward, struggling between hope and fear."

Spring found Narcissa at Fort Vancouver, again under the friendly roof of Dr. and Mrs. McLoughlin. Her spirits were renewed by two months' visit there and by further weeks as guest at the Methodist mission on the Willamette. She must have felt as if she were back in her beloved Steuben County that summer among her own kind of people. But eventually she had to return to fear and "moral darkness."

During Narcissa's stay on the Willamette, the "Great Migration" of 1843 got under way, with perhaps a thousand men, women and children, and their livestock and wagons. Marcus Whitman, returning from Boston, came upon the throng at the Missouri and served as a guide across the plains and mountains.

When this tide of settlers had passed on toward the Willamette Valley, few supplies remained at Waiilatpu. It was a bleak prospect to which Narcissa returned. Every fall during the next four years, another settler horde moved in. Many of the immigrants had to be housed and fed for extended periods. Marcus and Narcissa even adopted the seven Sager children whose parents had died on the trail. The work was unending for the once-sturdy doctor and his now-fading wife.

Now, Tilaukait and one of his followers, Tomahas ("The Murderer"), stirred up their tribesmen against the missionaries. They asserted, with some truthfulness, that the streams of white people were a threat to Indian ownership of the land. Also Joe Lewis, a half-breed, and an educated Delaware named Tom Hill agitated among both the Cayuses and the Nez Perces, describing the fate of the Indians east of the Rockies after the missionaries had come among them.

In 1847, the immigrants brought an epidemic of measles. Both whites and Indians were taken ill, and Marcus attended them all, hardly sleeping for days and nights on end. Having no immunity to the disease, the Indians, especially the children, suffered much more severely than the whites. More than half the tribe died. Most of the whites survived.

Joe Lewis told the Cayuses that Whitman was poisoning

the Indians. The white people got well and the Indians died, he said. The medicine the white doctor gave the Indian children must be poison.

There was not much rest on the Sabbath, November 28, 1847, for either Marcus or Narcissa. All day, the exhausted woman cared for the desperately ill Helen Meek and Louise Sager. Directing the mission, where some sixty persons now lived, took every last ounce of her strength.

Near midnight Marcus came home from a two-day ride to the Umatilla where he had gone to treat sick Indians. He was extremely weary and deeply troubled. He sat by the stove in the sitting room and spoke to his wife in guarded tones.

His old friend Stickus, from whom he had borrowed a mule at Umatilla, had whispered an ominous warning. Joe Lewis was urging the Cayuses to kill him as an unsuccessful *tewat* of their own race would be killed. If Narcissa slept at all that night, it must have been to dream fitfully of disaster.

Marcus watched over the sick children. He did not lie down at all, despite his weariness.

Dawn of Monday, November 29, was bleak. Fog shrouded the mission and the Cayuse lodges. Occasionally the gray mantle dissolved into a cold drizzle. In the mission yard, two of the white men killed a beef, as surly Indians stood watching. Narcissa filled a tub with warm water to bathe one of the children.

It was nearly noon when an Indian came to inform the doctor that a son of Chief Tilaukait had died and was being taken to the burial ground. The chief had already lost two children to the measles epidemic. Dr. Whitman must have felt the hostility as he read the Scriptures in the fog over the grave of Tilaukait's son.

In early afternoon, Narcissa came from the pantry, with a cup of milk for one of the children, and met Tilaukait and Tomahas face to face in the kitchen. They asked roughly to speak to her husband. She was terrified. She moved quickly to the sitting room where the doctor was preparing medicine. She closed the door and bolted it, then told Marcus in a frightened voice that the two Indians were there to see him.

Marcus went out to face his enemies. Narcissa locked the door after him. No one knows what Tilaukait said to the white man, but while they conversed Tomahas struck Marcus on the head with a tomahawk. John Sager, who was in the kitchen winding twine, tried to reach a pistol on the wall, but Tilaukait drew a rifle from under his blanket and shot the young man dead.

Whitman struggled with Tomahas through the outside kitchen door. There he fell from another blow of the hatchet. Tilaukait's rifle then inflicted a mortal wound in the doctor's throat as he lay in the mud.

Marcus did not die at once. Narcissa, hearing the shot, rushed through the kitchen and gathered him in her arms. With the help of other women of the mission who had come running she dragged him into the sitting room and laid him on a settee. Narcissa got ashes from the fireplace with which to stanch the blood gushing from the doctor's wound.

"Do you know me?" Narcissa asked her dying husband.

"Yes," he replied.

"Can you speak to me?"

"No," he said almost inaudibly.

The attack had been well planned. While Tilaukait and Tomahas were disposing of Dr. Whitman and John Sager, other Indians took up positions. Most of the men working about the mission were picked off, one by one. Nathan Kimball, who had been butchering the beef, and Andrew Rodgers, the teacher, came running wounded to the house and were admitted by Narcissa. Then, as she stood by the now glassless door, a shot rang out from the top of a haystack. Narcissa fell, a wound in her arm.

"Oh, what will become of my little ones!" exclaimed Narcissa. "Lord, save these little ones!" she prayed.

All in the house sought safety upstairs. Soon the Indians invaded the house and broke the door to the stairway. Rodgers pointed a broken gun over the banister and the Indians withdrew.

"For the space of an hour," wrote Catherine Sager many years later, "all was still as death except the low voice of Mr. R. engaged in prayer for the safety of all."

Providence was not to grant the wish. After a time, an Indian came to the foot of the stairs, protesting friendship. Other Indians, he said, planned to burn the house, but the people in the upper rooms would be escorted safely to one of the other buildings if they came down.

"God has raised us up a friend," said Narcissa, as Rodgers helped her down the stairs and placed her on a settee, like the one on which her husband was lying, still breathing but unconscious. Rodgers took one end of the settee and a Mrs. Hayes the other. They carried the wounded woman into the yard. Their appearance was a signal for further bloodshed. Shadowy savages raised guns to their shoulders. Rodgers fell, dropping his end of the settee. Narcissa, who had been struck again by at least two bullets, rolled from the makeshift litter. One of the Indians lifted her head by its golden hair and struck her in the face.

Narcissa was the only woman killed in the massacre. Eleven men, besides Dr. Whitman, were slain. Louise Sager and Helen Meek succumbed from lack of medical attention. Six persons escaped to spread word of the murders, and after a month of frightening uncertainty, Peter Skene Ogden, now factor at Fort Vancouver, came to ransom the thirty-four children, eight women and five men the Indians held as hostages. The Hudson's Bay man bought their freedom with five hundred dollars worth of guns, blankets, shirts and trinkets.

The massacre ended for many years all missionary work east of the Cascades, although Henry Spalding was to return in later life to preach again to the Nez Perces. Eliza, however, died within a few years on the Willamette.

Five Indians, including Tilaukait and Tomahas, were hanged at Oregon City on June 3, 1850, with Joe Meek, first United States marshal of Oregon Territory, as hangman. The massacre had hastened the establishment of the United States government in the Pacific Northwest.

A column marks the spot in the southeastern Washington wheat country where Waiilatpu stood. The United States government has made it a national monument. A college, a county and a national forest bear the name of the rugged, courageous doctor and his fair-haired wife.

Peace has long reigned at the Place of the Rye Grass, the kind of peace that would have set Narcissa's golden voice singing praises to the Lord. A statue of Marcus Whitman stands in Statuary Hall in the Capitol Building in Washington, D.C., but in the hearts of northwesterners Narcissa stands even taller than he. The life-loving woman of Angelica did not turn back even in the face of death.

3 · JOSEPH L. MEEK—
RAGGED "ENVOY EXTRAORDINARY"

Everybody laughed at big, burly Joe Meek, and that's what he wanted folks to do. He would rather tell stories—richly embellished ones about his experiences as a mountain man— than do most anything else, especially plowing.

His dark eyes would twinkle and his round, jovial face would beam as he told, for instance, of the time he and another trapper named Reese fell asleep while on night guard duty in Blackfoot country. Captain William Sublette had a method of signaling his guards. Every now and then during the night he called out, "All's well!" The guards were to respond with the same words. This night he received no reply.

"Sublette came round the horse pen swearin' and snortin'," recalled Joe, chuckling. "He was powerful mad. Before he got to whar Reese war, he made so much noise that he waked him; and Reese, in a loud whisper, called to him, 'Down, Billy! Injuns!' Sublette got down on his belly mighty quick. 'What? Whar?' he asked.

" 'They war right thar when you hollered so,' said Reese.

" 'Whar is Meek?' whispered Sublette.

" 'He's trying to shoot one,' answered Reese, still in a whisper. Reese then crawled over to whar I war, and told me what had been said, and informed me what to do. In a few minutes I crawled cautiously over to Reese's post. Sublette asked me how many Injuns had been thar, and I told him I couldn't make out the number. In the morning a pair of Injun moccasins war found, which I had taken care to leave thar. Our story got us the credit of vigilance, instead of our receiving our just dues for neglect of duty."

Such stories, told around a mountain man's campfire, or in a warm buffalo-skin lodge on a winter evening, or later in a farmer's log shanty in the Willamette Valley, were greeted with roars of laughter. Six-foot-two Meek would double over in mirth at his own humor, slapping his knees and roaring even louder than his audience.

Joe was a natural-born showman. Contemporaries described his voice as melodious and well modulated, though he spoke all his life in a backwoods dialect. Besides telling stories, he liked to ride and shoot and shout like a wild Indian. Eleven years in the mountains had made him more like an Indian than a white man. He was alert to every rustle that signaled the presence of human or animal foe.

Joe Meek might have stayed in the Rockies till he died. He liked it there. Even as a boy back in Virginia he had shunned farm work. He preferred hunting and fishing to school. Trapping beaver and fighting Indians, going for long stretches without food or water, were no life for a lazy man, but it was an exciting life and suited Joe's temperament perfectly. Camp keepers and squaws did the tedious work; and in the winter a trapper and hunter had lots of time to sit around the lodges spinning yarns with such men as Kit Carson, Jim Bridger and Robert "Doc" Newell. In his first winter in the mountains, young Meek even read some books—supplied by Jedediah Smith's small library.

From the year he celebrated his nineteenth birthday until 1840—a span of eleven years—Joe Meek fought and trapped, hunted and yarned in the Rockies, when he wasn't out hunting beaver elsewhere. Every summer he showed up at rendezvous to trade his peltries for the mountain man's necessities and luxuries. He did well at it, too, if one can believe his description of the things he bought for his first wife, a Snake Indian woman called the Lamb of the Mountains.

Meek's biographer, Mrs. Frances Fuller Victor, quotes Joe on how much he paid to deck out his bride and her horse in highest rendezvous style (Mrs. Victor tidied up Joe's language; he never spoke that way):

She was the most beautiful Indian woman I ever saw . . . and when she was mounted on her dapple gray horse, which cost me three hundred dollars, she made a fine show. She wore a skirt of beautiful blue broadcloth, and a bodice and leggings of scarlet cloth, of the very finest make. Her hair was braided and fell over her shoulders, a scarlet silk handkerchief, tied on hood fashion, covered her head; and the finest embroidered moccasins her feet. She rode like all the Indian women, astride, and carried on one side of the saddle the tomahawk for war, and on the other the pipe of peace. The name of her horse was "All Fours." His accoutrements were as fine as his rider's. The saddle, crupper, and bust girths cost one hundred and fifty dollars; the bridle fifty dollars; and the musk-a-moots fifty dollars more. All these articles were ornamented with fine cut glass beads, porcupine quills, and hawk's bells, that tinkled at every step. Her blankets were of scarlet and blue, and of the finest quality. Such was the outfit of the trapper's wife, *Umentucken, Tukutey, Undenwatsy,* the Lamb of the Mountains.

Umentucken died young. A stray Bannock arrow pierced her heart in one of the many Indian skirmishes in which her husband was involved. Joe's second wife was a Nez Perce woman, who bore him a daughter, the Helen Mar Meek who died of measles at Waiilatpu after the Whitman massacre. This woman left him to return to her own people. His third wife was also a Nez Perce; he called her Virginia. She went with him to the Willamette Valley and long outlived him. A daughter of Chief Kowesote, Virginia was only fifteen when

Joe met and wooed her. Two of her sisters married Joe's trapper friends, "Doc" Newell and Caleb Wilkins.

Though Joe was extremely fond of the Rockies, he did not spend all of his time there while in the fur trade. He made a trip across the Sierra Nevada to California and back. In the desert west of the Great Salt Lake, he lived, like the Digger Indians, on insects.

"I held my hands in an ant hill until they war covered with ants, then greedily licked them off," Joe recalled. "I took the soles off my moccasins, crisped them in the fire and ate them. In our extremity, the large black crickets which are found in this country war considered game. We used to take a kettle of hot water, catch the crickets and throw them in, and when they stopped kicking, eat them. That war not what we called *'cant tickup ko hanch'* (Shoshone for 'good meat, my friend'), but it kept us alive."

His travels took him far to the southeast also, to near the Cimarron River where Jedediah Smith was killed. There Joe, Kit Carson and four others ran into a large Comanche war party. No cover of any kind was available to protect them against the much larger force of savages. So they made a "fort" of dead mules.

The trappers had seven mules which they killed by slashing their throats. Holding on to the dying animals, the men made them fall in a circle. The scent of fresh blood caused the Comanches' horses to rear and turn back before the Indians came within spear-throwing range. The trappers fired three guns at a time, while the others were reloaded, and after a time the Indians withdrew. Even so the Carson-Meek party nearly died of sunstroke and thirst before they found their way back to camp seventy-five miles distant.

The rendezvous of 1839 was the last one held in the Rockies. There was some trading in furs at the posts that had sprung up, but the glory days of the mountain men were past. Joe stuck it out for another year, but he found the beaver scarce. He could have bought no belled and beaded saddle for a wife that year. He had barely enough clothes to be decent when he wound up in September, 1840, at Fort Hall, near present Pocatello, Idaho.

"Doc" Newell, his brother-in-law, had left word at Bear River for Joe to meet him at Fort Hall, where Meek's wife and baby were also staying.

"The fur trade is dead," said Newell. "We cannot return to the States. Let's go down to the Willamette and take farms."

"I'll go where you do, Newell," replied Meek. "What suits you, suits me."

Several wagons had collected at Fort Hall. Missionaries and other travelers had abandoned them there, trading them to trappers for guide service over the rest of the Oregon Trail to the Snake and Columbia. Newell decided the group would take three of these wagons all the way to the Columbia, the first of hundreds that were to follow in the next few years.

Besides the three brothers-in-law—Newell, Meek and Caleb Wilkins—there were several others in the caravan. Meek, Wilkins and a man named Nicholas drove the wagons, and "Doc" Newell rode ahead as the leader.

Sagebrush as high as the horses' heads, lava beds, streams and canyons made the journey difficult, just as they had for Marcus Whitman four years earlier. The men had to discard the wagon beds, but the wheels rolled on. And they continued to roll beyond Fort Boise, where Whitman had been forced to give up his wagon, over the thickly wooded and steep Blue Mountains into the yard at Waiilatpu. There Marcus and Narcissa Whitman greeted them cordially, killing a fat hog in their honor. The kindly missionaries took in Joe's emaciated and half-wild daughter, Helen Mar, whom he had picked up along the way and taken with him so that she might have the advantages due the daughter of a white man.

The Cayuses were wonder-struck by the wagons, which they called "horse canoes." Dr. Whitman was delighted that the trappers had beaten his efforts as a teamster. He assured the men they would never regret bringing the wagons with them, despite all the trouble they had encountered.

"You have broken the ice," Whitman told Newell. "When others see that wagons have passed, they too will pass, and in a few years the valley will be full of our people."

The mountain men left the wagons at Fort Walla Walla and continued the journey to the Willamette on horseback. There they spent a miserable first winter in unaccustomed rain, with little more than boiled wheat to eat. Game was scarce in this country; a man couldn't shoot his dinner whenever his stomach demanded food.

Big-hearted Dr. John McLoughlin, chief factor at Fort Vancouver, helped most of the mountain men, as he helped other settlers, with seed and livestock to get them started as farmers. But the serious-minded Hudson's Bay man did not take to the fun-loving Meek. Joe often visited the post on the Columbia, spinning his yarns, laughing and loafing. Dr. McLoughlin told him to "leave off killing Indians and go to work." The ragged clown paid little heed to the advice, and McLoughlin, as a consequence, declined to lend Joe the necessities he freely offered to others.

Yet even with the help from Vancouver, the settlers had a hard time making ends meet. The mountain men chose for their farms the treeless Tualatin Plains near present Hillsboro, Oregon. One reason may have been that it took less work to bring such land into cultivation than other soil which required the felling of giant fir trees and removal of stumps. Peter H. Burnett, who was to become the first governor of

California, was as bad off as the rest of them.

One of Meek's favorite stories involved Burnett and a pumpkin. The neighbors were traveling to Willamette Falls (Oregon City) with a wagon load of wheat to be ground into flour. Burnett had only a little bread with him for his supper. Joe brought a large bundle wrapped in a blanket. Burnett was hopeful that Meek had a haunch of venison in the package, and his fellow traveler didn't disillusion him. But when the bearded giant unwrapped it there was only a large pumpkin.

"What! Is that all we have for supper?" cried the disappointed Burnett.

"Roast punkin ain't so bad," chuckled Meek. "It's buffalo tongue compared to ants or moccasin soles."

Joe liked to tell, too, how he got a cow from the mission farm at Champoeg. Mr. Whitcom, the farm manager, advised Meek to pray for a cow if he wanted one.

"I can't pray," said Joe. "That's your business."

The pious missioner insisted it was every man's duty to pray for himself. "How do you expect to get what you want, if you don't ask for it?" he said.

"I did ask," answered Joe. "I asked you."

"You must ask God," said Whitcom.

"Tell you what I'll do," Joe replied. "If you'll furnish the cow, I'll pray right har for half an hour." And he did. Afterward the cow's milk made the boiled wheat taste much better.

Meek did a lot of traveling around and everybody got to know him. One fancies they enjoyed seeing him ride up on his mule. There were few things to laugh about on the frontier in those days, and the happy giant always had a fund of stories to make an isolated settler momentarily forget his troubles. This "politicking" accounted for his selection as sheriff and the crowning honor of his life—his election as envoy to the Congress and the President of the United States.

On the night of May 1, 1843, Joe was telling stories to American and French-Canadian settlers at Champoeg, which lies on the right bank of the Willamette River midway between Oregon City and Salem. The tall ex-trapper was dressed in ragged buckskins, the same he had worn when he left the Rockies nearly three years earlier, except for a handsome vest. This he had picked up somewhere while riding his mule around the countryside when he should have been plowing.

Between yarns, Joe was talking up a report a committee was to make the next day. The report recommended the formation of a provisional government looking toward Oregon's becoming a territory of the United States. The death of another former trapper, Ewing Young, had presented the settlers with the problem of probating the estate. Also wolves had been raiding the settlers' livestock, and meetings had been held to seek some way of collecting money to pay bounties for wolf hides. The Hudson's Bay Company and the Methodist mission near Salem were no longer adequate agencies for solving the increasing problems brought about by the coming of settlers. A government was needed.

Other men circulated that night at Champoeg. They found many of the assembled people receptive to the idea of forming a government. Even some of the French-Canadians who had retired from service with the Hudson's Bay Company were willing to organize, though this would mean a further lessening of British and Canadian claims on the Oregon Country. The Americans were certain they had more than enough votes to carry the proposal next day.

However, something went wrong. After the committee's report had been read and speeches delivered, including a short oration by Joe Meek, a motion was made to adopt the report. Instead of loud acclaim, as had been expected, the

"Nays" rang out louder than the "Yeas." George Le Breton, one of the committee members, moved for a division of the house so that a count could be made of the voters. But by now the assembly was in confusion. Some had wandered out of the rude Hudson's Bay granary to the open meadow. The interests of America required a stronger voice than Le Breton's.

Up jumped black-haired, black-bearded Joe Meek in his ragged buckskins and fancy vest. With a shout that would have been heard at the height of festivities at a mountain men's rendezvous, Joe cried out:

"Who's for a divide! All in favor of the report, and for an organization, follow me!"

Quickly order came out of confusion. The Americans and some of the French-Canadians followed the tall, dark man in the vest. The others, without a leader, lined up on the other side of the chairman. Tradition has it that when the count was made there were fifty-two for organization and fifty against. However, the official minutes did not include the tally.

In any case, the settlers of Oregon voted for a government of their own, based on that of the United States, in the hope that closer ties would follow, as they did.

"Three cheers for our side!" yelled Joe when the count was announced.

The government organization was completed on July 5, and Joe Meek was selected to serve as sheriff of all the country from California to an undetermined boundary with Canada and from the summit of the Rocky Mountains to the Pacific Ocean. He was the law in a region larger than Texas. Joe must have let out another whoop or two when that vote was announced.

Tragedy—the Whitman massacre—led to Meek's sensational sojourn in the nation's capital.

The legislature, of which he was a member, had just assembled in Oregon City in early December, 1847, when word came of the slaying of Dr. and Mrs. Whitman and several others at the Waiilatpu Mission far up the Columbia. Joe and nearly every other man in the House felt a personal loss. The Whitmans had succored many of them near the end of the long trail to the Willamette Valley. Joe's own daughter, Helen Mar, was living with the Whitmans.

Had she been killed, too? Would the Cayuse uprising set other Indian tribes on the warpath? The little group of men at Oregon City was deeply troubled.

A resolution was immediately passed directing the governor to raise and equip a company of riflemen to be sent to The Dalles to protect the settlements. Next order of business was the sending of a messenger to Washington to urge the United States to extend its protection to the settlers in the Oregon Country. Only the year before, the boundary line had been determined by agreement with the British. All of the Pacific Northwest to the 49th parallel now was U.S. territory, but nothing had been done to protect it.

Actually two messengers were sent. Governor George Abernethy, without consulting the legislature, assigned J. Quinn Thornton to go by ship. The legislature, on the other hand, chose Sheriff Joe Meek.

Joe, no doubt, had told his fellow legislators that he was a cousin of President James K. Polk. One cannot imagine his neglecting such a subject for boastful conversation. In truth, he was related to the President. With entree to the White House and as an official of the provisional government who knew better than most men the tricky trails of winter in the mountains, Meek was the logical choice.

For a man of action, the sheriff of the great Northwest was rather slow getting started across the continent. Skirmishes between the militiamen and the Cayuses helped delay him.

At Waiilatpu, Meek found the buildings burned and the bodies of the massacre victims scattered about the yard. Wolves had dug up the remains of the Whitmans and the others, including Meek's own daughter. Sentimentally, he cut off a lock of Narcissa Whitman's blond hair as a keepsake. Then he helped rebury the bodies.

Members of the militia escorted across the Blue Mountains Meek, George Ebbert and several others who had chosen to join the hard winter trek. Then by themselves, the little group floundered through the deep snows in the Rockies. They stopped to rest occasionally with some of Joe's mountain friends and sometimes traveled at night to avoid hostile Indians. The Oregonians reached St. Joseph, Missouri, May 11, having traveled more than eighteen hundred miles in a little more than two months.

From there on, the trip was easier, except that Meek had no money to pay for his passage on steamers, stages and finally the steam cars. But Joe had a valuable resource, his mouth, and he put it to good use even in this more effete part of the country.

The St. Louis papers gave him a big play. The bearded giant in ragged, dirty buckskins and wolfskin cap became a sensation. Word spread rapidly by telegraph of the arrival of the emissary from distant Oregon who had so bravely crossed the mountains and plains in winter. His mission, to seek the protection of the United States government for citizens in the wilderness, became the subject of sympathetic conversation wherever newspapers circulated.

Two steamboats were at the docks in St. Louis preparing to leave for Pittsburgh. Joe instantly selected one of them, the *Declaration*. Climbing to her hurricane deck he roared to the crowd on shore: "This way, gentlemen, if you please. Come right on board the *Declaration*. I am the man from Oregon, with dispatches to the President of these United States, that you read about in this morning's paper. Come on board, ladies and gentlemen, if you want to hear the news from Oregon. . . . Passengers who come aboard the *Declaration* shall hear all about it before they get to Pittsburgh. . . ."

The *Declaration* got most of the business that trip, and Sheriff Meek of Oregon got a free ride and the best the galley could produce.

At Wheeling, he needed passage on the stage line to Cumberland, Maryland. The regular coach had already left, so Joe boldly asked for a special one.

"Who are you?" asked the startled manager.

"I am Envoy Extraordinary and Minister Plenipotentiary from the Republic of Oregon to the Court of the United States," said Joe, producing the letters addressed to the Congress and to President Polk.

The extra stage was produced, and as it jerked forward behind its whipped-up horses, Joe stuck his wolfskin-clad head out the window and whooped for the benefit of bystanders. At least, that's how he told it later.

The last leg of his journey was by train. When the conductor came around asking for the tickets, Joe pretended he couldn't understand, and answered in the language of the Snake Indians. His fellow passengers were in on the joke, and the conductor saw the humor, too, after a time, and let the Envoy Extraordinary ride free to Washington.

Joe had center stage in Washington, and he didn't underplay his part. He stopped at Coleman's Hotel for dinner on his way to the White House. His grimy buckskin outfit and his shaggy hair and beard made the people stare. By loud conversation with the Negro waiter he drew additional attention to himself. He asked the waiter to read the menu.

"People in my country can't read," Joe explained.

The waiter read and mentioned "game."

"What kind of game?" asked Joe.

"Small game, sir," said the waiter.

"Fetch me a piece of antelope," shouted the man from Oregon, and when the servant said he didn't know what that was, Joe explained: "In my country antelope and deer are small game; bear and buffalo are large game. I reckon if you haven't got one, you haven't got the other, either. Fetch me some beef."

After ordering a second helping of beef, Joe commented that it was better meat than the old mule he had eaten in the mountains. Before he left he told the waiter, loudly so all could hear, that he was "Envoy Extraordinary and Minister Plenipotentiary from the Republic of Oregon to the Court of the United States." Then he exited, as good actors do when they have delivered their punch lines.

At the White House it was old home week for the tattered "envoy." The mulatto doorman was a childhood playmate. The President's private secretary was Knox Walker, a relative of Meek's.

"Uncle Joe!" exclaimed Walker when he recognized the man behind the black beard. Then he reached out to greet the giant. "Take care, Knox!" said Joe. "Don't come too close. I'm ragged, dirty and lousy."

"Cousin James," the President, was equally cordial. He invited Joe to stay at the White House, and called for Mrs. Polk and another lady to come and meet the visitor.

"When I heard the silks rustling in the passage, I felt more frightened than if a hundred Blackfeet had whooped in my ear," Meek told his biographer many years later. He was not one to minimize either his fears or his valor.

Barbered and clothed in the mode of the day, Meek became

the toast of Washington. He met the important men of the Congress and the Cabinet. While J. Quinn Thornton sat in Congress as a delegate from Oregon, the now fashionable mountain man got around in the lobbies. Whether he or Thornton did more to win territorial status for the Oregon Country is debatable. In any event, the Congress in the last hours of its session, on August 14, 1848, passed a bill authorizing a territorial government.

Joe traveled to many cities of the North in the company of congressmen who were campaigning for re-election. The summer was one continuous "rendezvous" for the fun-loving, reluctant plowman from the Tualatin Plains. Feminine members of eastern society made as much of him as did the lawmakers.

One lady, at a reception, asked him if he was married. Joe replied he had a wife and several children.

"I should think your wife would be afraid of the Indians!" exclaimed the woman.

"Afraid of Indians?" said Meek. "Why, Ma'am, she *is* an Indian."

As soon as Congress had voted to make Oregon a territory, President Polk appointed General Joseph Lane of Indiana governor of the new addition to the nation. "Cousin Joe" Meek was named U.S. marshal.

In September, Lane, Meek, a company of riflemen and others—fifty-five persons in all—set out for Oregon from St. Louis, taking the Santa Fe Trail and pushing on to California. Most of the men deserted either along the trail or in California where the 1849 gold rush had started. In San Francisco, Meek met some two hundred Oregonians who had come south to make their fortunes.

The governor and marshal sailed north from San Francisco to Astoria on the ship *Jeanette,* then paddled 120 miles up the Columbia and Willamette to Oregon City. They arrived there on March 2, barely in time to proclaim the territorial government before President Polk's term of office ran out. Joe had brought back a government, but hardly an army to protect the settlers. Upon his arrival in Oregon only two of his soldiers were left.

Joe's old friends were startled at his transformation. Gone were the buckskin breeches and blanket capote. In their place were fashionable trousers and a coat with brass buttons. But Marshal Meek was the same man underneath, with a stock of new stories about hobnobbing with the President and congressmen in Washington. The stories improved with each telling.

Meek was a busy man the next few years, opening sessions of the court, helping take the census, serving official papers, hanging the Indians convicted of the Whitman murders and otherwise acting as Governor Lane's right-hand man. During his term of office Washington Territory was established. This made his domain much smaller than it had been originally. And when Franklin Pierce became President, Meek lost his job as marshal, though he served as deputy marshal on and off.

As deputy he wrote a report still in existence in the Washington County Courthouse at Hillsboro, Oregon. It set some kind of record for lawmen's misspellings.

On the back of a summons for David, James and Black Jack, Indians sought as witnesses, Joe reported as follows:

The within naimed Witeness caint Be found having gon Bare Hunting
September 28, 1854.
                    J. L. Meek
                    Deputy U. Staits Marshal

Meek later served as a major in the Indian Wars of 1855–56, though the title was no great joy to him since he already was known as "Colonel."

In 1870, Mrs. Victor's book, of which he was a sort of co-author, revived interest in the aging onetime "Envoy Extraordinary." But, generally speaking, Meek did not cut a very large figure after his term as marshal ran out. Racial prejudice arose as white wives among the settlers began to outnumber the Indian wives of the fur trappers. One of Meek's sons became a fugitive after a fatal fight brought on by such prejudice, even though he was finally cleared in a court of law. The new settlers were people of a different sort, farmers rather than mountain men, and somewhat more literate.

Yet, when Joe Meek's funeral was held on June 21, 1875, at his farm four miles north of Hillsboro, "400 or 500" persons attended. In a sparsely settled country, that was equivalent to an attendance of ten thousand or more today. As the correspondent for the *Portland Oregonian* put it next day, the people of Oregon appreciated his service to his territory and state, "notwithstanding the people of our country have been in the habit of looking on Colonel Meek as a man full of levity, too good natured to amount to much outside of being a good fellow in general. . . ."

He was a good fellow and a colorful one. Someday, maybe, television and the movies will discover him.

4 · MICHAEL T. SIMMONS AND GEORGE WASHINGTON BUSH, WHO WENT WHERE THEY WISHED

Some men came to hate each other on the long, hard journey over the Oregon Trail. But others became fast friends. Character weakness betrayed itself under the stress of hardship and frustration. But admirable traits of friendliness, generosity and loyalty became equally apparent.

One of the strangest and most lasting friendships developed during the migration of 1844. Damon and Pythias could hardly have been more loyal to one another than were Michael Troutman Simmons, a tall, young man of Irish descent, and George Washington Bush, a much older man whose dark skin denoted his mixed Negro and Caucasian ancestry. Both came from slave states, but there was no feeling of superiority or inferiority between them.

So strong was their friendship that it broke up a pattern for settlement of the Pacific Northwest that the Hudson's Bay Company and Dr. John McLoughlin, the company's representative at Fort Vancouver, had hoped would save western Washington for the British.

To many of the tatterdemalions who emerged from the trail Dr. McLoughlin must have looked like the Jehovah they read about in their dog-eared Bibles.

Standing over six feet tall, he towered majestically above ordinary men. A full head of silken white hair fell to his shoulders. He was at once generous and stern, and not infrequently his cold, blue eyes blazed up in righteous anger.

Fort Vancouver, after the mountains and deserts, must have looked like Heaven. Even in Missouri where the trek had begun many months back, few places could be considered its equal. Broad fields, full of grain and potatoes, stretched from the Columbia over the knoll on which stood the stockade, the houses and store buildings. Beyond, fat livestock grazed in the pastures.

The "White-Headed Eagle" was mortal, of course. He was only a king—monarch of an empire that stretched from the Rockies to the sea and from Mexican California to the Arctic. The gold-headed cane he always carried might well have been his scepter. The rich furniture of his house befitted his station; it had been shipped around Cape Horn from London.

It was small wonder then that the ragged, penniless men who straggled down the river with their families and worn-out cattle and horses did as they were told by the Hudson's Bay factor. One does not ordinarily challenge a king. They were dependent on McLoughlin's generosity both for food and for the essential tools they needed to start afresh in the new country. And the Eagle was generous. Too much so, complained his superiors on far-off Hudson Bay and in London. Over the years, he advanced thousands of dollars worth of goods to the newcomers, much of which was never repaid. Sometimes, after the settlers had lost some of their awe of him—when they had discovered he was neither Jehovah nor actually a king—they repaid his favors with recriminations.

What the giant of Vancouver told the immigrants to do was to their advantage. Go south, he said, to the Willamette Valley, the largest river basin north of California. The climate and the soil were excellent. Americans had settled there already in considerable numbers and had founded schools and churches. Commerce was developing among the people of like traditions who made splendid neighbors on whom to call

for help and sociability. North of the Columbia, said Mc-
Loughlin, was wilderness, inhabited only by Indians and a
few Hudson's Bay men. That was no place to seek a home.

So the settlers dutifully crossed the Columbia and found
homesteads for themselves in the rich Willamette Valley or
on the Tualatin Plains.

Thus, for a long time, the Eagle kept the British aerie free
of intruders. If Americans stayed out of the country north
and west of the Columbia River there still was hope that its
thick fir forests and the incomparable Puget Sound could be
preserved for the Crown and the Hudson's Bay Company.

Then came the migration of 1844 and with it stubborn
young Michael Simmons and dark-skinned George Bush. To
them McLoughlin was neither Jehovah nor a monarch.

By the autumn of 1844 the "king" of Oregon had lost some
of his authority. The settlers in the Willamette had formed
a provisional government and were expecting an answer soon
from Washington, D.C., to their petitions for territorial status.
But the man at Fort Vancouver retained plenty of authority
still, and his hopes remained strong that what is now the western two-thirds of Washington State would continue to rest in
British hands. The border had not yet been determined, and
until it was he would continue to send the Americans south to
the Willamette.

Dr. McLoughlin almost succeeded, too, this year as he
had in the past. Only a tall, lanky, thirty-year-old white man
from Kentucky and an elderly colored man from Missouri
rejected his counsel. "Colonel" Simmons had been second
in command of the wagon train. Bush, who was surprisingly
well-to-do from cattle trading in Missouri, had come to the
assistance of some of his white fellow travelers. By so doing
he had won many friends. Simmons was especially fond of
him.

Simmons and Bush received the usual advice from the

dignified and towering factor. Joining in, every now and then, was James Douglas, McLoughlin's dark, young assistant, who soon would succeed the Eagle as chief at Fort Vancouver and who eventually would become Sir James Douglas, governor of Vancouver Island and British Columbia. But Simmons and Bush seemed singularly unimpressed by the well-reasoned arguments in favor of the Willamette Valley.

The icy eyes of the Eagle may have blazed a little as he realized that this pair of newcomers were not about to set off across the river. Instead, they and several others moved up the Columbia a few miles, still on the north shore, and established a camp for the winter on the Washougal. A few weeks later, Dr. McLoughlin received reports that Simmons and five other men were poking about on the Cowlitz, still north of the Columbia, evidently trying to find a way to Puget Sound.

The upshot was that Simmons and Bush, plus a few other pioneers and their families who had accompanied them across the plains, became the first American settlers on the sound, the great arm of the Pacific that McLoughlin had hoped to keep inviolate.

There were two good reasons why Simmons and Bush had been adamant against settling in the Willamette Valley.

As a mulatto, Bush had already seen enough of racial prejudice. He had left Missouri to escape the slurs inflicted on himself and his white wife and five children because of his color. Then on reaching Oregon he learned that only the previous June the Provisional Legislative Committee, while rejecting slavery, had also prohibited free Negroes or mulattoes. He was not going to submit again to such discrimination after traveling more than two thousand miles to escape it. As a free man who had fought with General Andrew Jackson at New Orleans he felt he was entitled to all the rights and privileges enjoyed by fair-skinned Americans.

Then too, the thin, tall Simmons was a man of rare independence. He was also a shrewd leader. His companions recognized this and made him colonel of the wagon train. Simmons was unlettered but not unenlightened, as one biographer put it.

McLoughlin's admonition not to settle north of the Columbia aroused in the young man from Kentucky a sort of contrariness, perhaps inherited from his Irish ancestors. He had planned, in fact, to settle in the Rogue River valley of southern Oregon, but now his loyalty to Bush and his natural stubbornness exerted themselves. If Hudson's Bay was so anxious that Americans should not settle north of the Columbia, he meant to find out more about that country. He was not a man to knuckle under to a foreign king or a fur-company baron. Besides, Bush could not accept the status decreed for his race by the legislature.

Therefore, in December, Simmons started down the Columbia to the Cowlitz, which flows into the great River of the West near where Longview and Kelso, Washington, now stand. There he and his companions struck into the interior, paddling and poling their frail boats against a strong current made almost unbreastable by heavy winter rains. In some places the Cowlitz was completely blocked by logs and driftwood. There the men were forced to carry their canoes and gear around the blockades through almost impenetrable timber and brush. They had traveled about thirty or forty miles up the stream when their provisions began to give out. So they had to turn around and head back for Vancouver. But Simmons would soon return.

During the long journey across the plains, Bush had been mulling over in his mind what he might do if racial prejudice in Oregon proved to be as strong as it had been in Missouri. John Minto, also an immigrant of 1844, tells in his reminiscences of a conversation with the Negro near Soda Springs on the western slope of the continental divide. Striking ahead of his party, Minto came upon Bush, who was traveling alone at the time. Minto wrote many years later:

Not many men left a slave state so well to do, and so generally respected, but it was not in the nature of things that he should be permitted to forget his color. As we went along together, he riding a mule and I on foot, he led the conversation to this subject. He told me he should watch, when we got to Oregon, what usage was awarded people of his color, and if he could not have a free man's rights he would seek the protection of the Mexican government in California or New Mexico. He said there were few in the train he would say as much to as he had just said to me. I told him I understood. This conversation enabled me afterwards to understand the chief reason for Colonel M.T. Simmons and his kindred, and Bush and [Gabriel] Jones determining to settle north of the Columbia. It was understood that Bush was assisting at least two of these to get to Oregon, and while they were all Americans, they would take no part in ill treating G.W. Bush on account of his color. . . .

Why the dark-skinned Missourian did not go south to California or some other Mexican refuge is not clear. Possibly he realized it was a matter of only a short time until California and New Mexico would become American territory, as indeed they did within four years. Perhaps he felt he would be safe from prejudice on distant Puget Sound in the midst of his friends of the trail. There was the possibility that when the border between Canada and the United States was agreed upon, the present western Washington would definitely become British territory, and, thus, would be less affected by the slavery question and its attendant abuses of freemen of color.

In theory, the country north of the Columbia was as subject to the law against Negroes and mulattoes as was the Willamette Valley. The provisional government pretended to rule all the country north to the parallel of 54 degrees, 40 minutes, the southern boundary of Russian America (Alaska). But, since there were no Americans living north of the river, the provisional government did not actually control that country. The Hudson's Bay Company was still supreme there.

This situation was not long to continue. In June, 1846, less than two years after Simmons and Bush arrived at Fort Vancouver, the boundary question was settled. President James K. Polk retreated from the position expressed so firmly in his campaign slogan of 1844: "Fifty-four Forty or Fight!" The British compromised on their claim to the country north and west of the Columbia River. The boundary was fixed at the 49th parallel, the same line that separates the countries between the Great Lakes and the Rockies.

This peaceful settlement did not come without crisis. In 1845, when Simmons and Bush were pushing northward to the sound, war seemed imminent. British warships visited both Puget Sound and the Columbia River. Two British Army lieutenants and one Navy officer spied out the country while traveling incognito, ostensibly on Hudson's Bay Company business. The spies decided that the land would be difficult to hold. American troops could pour across the plains and mountains even more easily than American settlers and in greater numbers. Besides, Sir John Gordon, captain of the warship *America*, didn't think the country was worth fighting for. He decided this from casual observation from the decks of his vessel, and he so reported to his brother, Lord Aberdeen, the British Foreign Secretary.

Thus, George Washington Bush did not long escape the rule of the race-conscious settlers south of the Columbia.

It worked out all right, though. His friend Simmons was elected to the Oregon Territorial Legislature and pushed through a bill exempting Bush and his family from the law against Negroes and mulattoes, and Congress by special act gave him 640 acres of land.

It is incomprehensible today how such a law as that adopted by the provisional lawmakers could have appeared in the code of a humane, democratic community. But it must be remembered that slavery was the nation's most controversial question at that time. The delay in admitting Oregon as a territory was due chiefly to the stalemate in Congress over whether new territories should be free or slave. There were a few slaves in Oregon; they had been brought in by their southern masters. These the legislative committee ruled must be removed from the country or set free. But the lawmakers went further in trying to avoid the whole race problem: they ordered that free Negroes and mulattoes must also depart.

Section 4 of the act read:

That when any free negro or mulatto shall have come to Oregon, he or she, as the case may be, if of the age of eighteen or upward, shall remove from and leave the country within the term of two years for males and three years for females from the passage of this act; and if any free negro or mulatto shall hereafter come to Oregon, if of the age aforesaid, he or she shall quit and leave within the term of two years for males and three years for females from his or her arrival in the country.

Section 6 provided:

That if any such free negro or mulatto shall fail to quit the country as required by this act, he or she may be arrested upon a warrant issued by some justice of the peace, and if guilty upon trial before such justice, shall receive upon his or her bare back not less than twenty nor more than thirty-nine stripes, to be inflicted by the constable of the proper county.

Such whippings, the act went on to say, should be inflicted every six months, so long as the violator remained in the country.

To the credit of the Willamette settlers, the law was never enforced and was soon repealed. But it is clear why George Bush did not take his family to the Willamette Valley. Imagine how a man would feel living under the threat of a whipping every six months just because his skin was dark!

Despite their rejection of Dr. McLoughlin's advice, men of the Simmons party were not ill-treated by the company during the winter. They obtained some work splitting shingles and hauling logs out of the nearby forests. They were tight-lipped about their future plans but the company agents were suspicious of them. The Hudson's Bay men continued to applaud the Willamette and degrade the country north of the Columbia as a place for American settlements. This only strengthened Simmons' resolve to make his home on Puget Sound. Bush declared that he, at least, must go there. His white friends remained loyal to him.

Simmons stayed near Fort Vancouver until after his fifth child, Christopher Columbus Simmons, was born. This was on April 10, 1845. Little Chris was the first American child born in what is now western Washington.

In July, Michael took leave of his wife, his newborn child and four older sons. With eight other Americans he retraced his route of the previous December, down the Columbia and up the Cowlitz. At the forks of the latter stream, the group pushed into the forests. At Cowlitz Prairie, near present Toledo, they hired as a guide a former Hudson's Bay employe, Peter Bercier. They learned that another American, John R. Jackson, had already been that way. He had located a claim on Cowlitz Prairie but had gone back to Oregon City to get his livestock and other possessions. Jackson's claim, however, was a considerable distance from Puget Sound.

With Bercier's help, the Americans continued northward through the deep forests and across small prairies, blazing the Cowlitz Trail. After many days of hard travel they reached Budd Inlet at the southern end of Puget Sound where the Washington State capitol dome is now reflected in the sparkling water.

In canoes, Simmons and his companions explored the shores of the sound, including Whidbey Island and Skagit Bay. But these did not appeal as much to the Kentuckian as did the falls on the Deschutes River, called "tum tum" by the Indians. The tall explorer had owned and operated a gristmill in Missouri, where he had lived for four years, and he shrewdly perceived that the water power in the falls of the Deschutes could make him a prosperous miller on this new frontier.

Simmons and his friends, having seen the land Hudson's Bay wished to keep from them, hastened back to Vancouver for their families. Before the year had run its course, the first Americans would be living on the shore of Puget Sound, laying the groundwork for the cities—Seattle, Tacoma, Olympia, etc.—which today make this section of the Pacific Northwest the richest and most populous.

But if the Americans had expected Dr. McLoughlin to bear them a grudge, they were pleasantly surprised. When the thirty men, women and children left Vancouver in September for Puget Sound to make their permanent settlement they carried with them a letter from the "Eagle" to Dr. William

F. Tolmie, who had charge of the Hudson's Bay Company post at Fort Nisqually, only a few miles east of the place Simmons had selected.

McLoughlin wrote to Tolmie that if he had any grain and potatoes to spare he should let Simmons have what he needed and to charge the cost to Fort Vancouver.

"They have conducted themselves in the most neighborly, friendly manner," said McLoughlin of the American invaders, "and I beg to recommend them to your kind assistance and friendly offices."

Company records show that Dr. Tolmie was indeed both kind and friendly. The settlers obtained 200 bushels of wheat at 80 cents a bushel, 100 bushels of peas for a total of $100, 300 bushels of potatoes at 50 cents a bushel and ten head of cattle at $12 a head. They could have expected no greater consideration if they had settled on the Willamette, as McLoughlin wished. Maybe the home office was right when it charged the Vancouver man with being too friendly to Americans.

Although by now Simmons and several of his companions knew well the route to Puget Sound, the trip north still was a difficult one. The men literally had to cut a road through the timber between the Cowlitz and the sound. Fallen trees were chopped apart with axes, since they had no saws, to permit their one wagon and several sleds to go through. Sometimes they built crude bridges over fallen trees. It took the party fifteen days to travel fifty-eight miles, the last several days in a drenching rain.

The settlers built a single cabin for communal living during the winter. Simmons didn't finish his own house until the following summer. But he was looking far into the future. Almost at once he laid out a townsite called New Market. Later it became known as Tumwater, from the Indian word for water, *tum—tum tum* for falling water. It is now a suburb of Olympia, the state capital, so called because of the sweeping view from the town of the Olympic Mountains across the sound.

Bush and some of the others settled a few miles south of the townsite on level ground known to this day as Bush Prairie. There he lived a happy life for near two decades, highly respected as one of the best farmers in the Pacific Northwest and as a good neighbor and host to wayfarers. His success as a farmer was demonstrated a few years after his death when his son, William Owen Bush, won the first premium at the Centennial Exposition in Philadelphia for wheat grown on Bush Prairie.

A story was told by a pioneer of how Bush thought more of his friends than of money. One winter the supply of grain was low on Puget Sound. Speculators cornered nearly all of the available wheat and the price soared skyward. Learning that the granaries on Bush Prairie were full, the profiteers offered to buy the grain from Bush at a large profit to him.

"I'll keep my grain," the aging man told the speculators, "so that my neighbors will have enough to live on and for seeding their fields in the spring. They have no money to pay your fancy prices, and I don't intend to see them want for anything I can provide them with."

Bush also got along well with the Indians, who undoubtedly felt a kinship for the man who, like themselves, had a skin of a different hue. One time two Indian tribes fought a battle on Bush Prairie. Before the battle, they agreed that no harm should come to the "whites" living there. Bush, of course, was included in this stipulation. On Puget Sound he had found the equal treatment he had traveled so far to seek.

The fugitive from prejudice died in 1863. If he was born in 1790, as some say, he was seventy-three when he passed on. But some sources give his birth year as 1778. If that were true, he would have been in his middle sixties when he crossed the plains, a remarkable accomplishment. In any case, the first Bush of Bush Prairie was an extraordinary man.

Simmons lost no time putting the water power of the Deschutes River to work. Using hand-hewn timbers and stones from the river bottom, he had a gristmill in operation by the fall of 1846.

Now the settlers could have bread. During the first year, they had eaten their wheat boiled, along with boiled peas, potatoes and fern roots. They had fared well, though. In addition to the staples obtained from Hudson's Bay, they had an abundance of game and fish. The shores of Puget Sound were rich in clams and other shellfish.

The market for lumber was even better than that for flour, so Mike Simmons immediately constructed a sawmill to be driven by the three waterfalls on his claim. Fort Nisqually was always in need of boards, but they still had to be made by hand. A pit was dug and one man got into it. A log was laid across the pit, and the man in the hole and another standing above pushed and pulled a saw until a board had been sliced from the log. This was slow, tedious work.

Several more Americans had straggled into the small community at the tip of Puget Sound, and eight of them joined Simmons in building the sawmill. A saw, discarded by the Hudson's Bay mill near Fort Vancouver, was purchased at 20 cents a pound. The blade was inserted in a frame that worked up and down through an arm attached to a water wheel. It was a crude mill, not much different from the pit mill at Nisqually, except that water power instead of Kanakas (Hawaiians) did the work. The lumber was sold at 75 cents per one hundred feet and was floated to Nisqually in rafts. A few years later, Simmons and two others built a sawmill on the site of present-day Tacoma.

The gold rush to California resulted in the establishment of the first American store on Puget Sound. And the store-keeper, naturally, was Michael T. Simmons. This store released the settlers from dependence on the Hudson's Bay Company, which had restricted their purchases to their actual needs, lest they begin trading with the Indians in competition with Hudson's Bay.

Edmund Sylvester, who owned the claims on Budd Inlet where Olympia now stands, was one of the many men from the Pacific Northwest who went to California to dig gold. He made a modest fortune there, and in the fall of 1849 purchased a small brig, the *Orbit*, in San Francisco with the thought of taking it north and obtaining a cargo of pilings, for which there was a big market in California. Simmons by now had sold his mills, and with the money thus obtained he bought a controlling interest in the *Orbit*, telling the captain to purchase a shipload of general merchandise in San Francisco so that he could start a store.

Sylvester was quick to see what a store might do for a town-site. So he built a two-story log structure in the still unsettled Olympia and gave it to Simmons with the understanding that he would open his store there. Next year another store was opened at Fort Steilacoom, a newly established military post. And in 1852, David Maynard, who had married Simmons' sister Catherine, after her husband died on the plains of cholera, took a shipload of cordwood to San Francisco and returned with a cargo of general merchandise. Simmons persuaded him to set up his shop on Elliott Bay to the north, rather than compete with him in Olympia. Maynard set out with an Indian friend, Chief Sealth, and, thus, a small struggling community later to be called Seattle, after the chief, got its first store.

Simmons' merchandising enterprise eventually went sour. A man he hired to keep his books and handle his affairs in San Francisco absconded. But the lanky Kentuckian remained an outstanding citizen.

During Simmons' first year in the West, the Oregon provisional legislature created a new county north of the Columbia, calling it Vancouver. It embraced all American territory north of the Columbia River and west of the Cascade Mountains. Mike Simmons, along with James Douglas of Hudson's Bay Company and Charles Forrest were named justices. John R. Jackson was made sheriff.

After Oregon Territory was established, including all the region west of the continental divide between California and the 49th parallel, Simmons was elected a member of the legislature. He represented all of what is now western Washington.

From 1850 to 1853, he served as postmaster at Olympia. The mail was brought to the sound by military couriers traveling between Vancouver and Fort Steilacoom. There were few letters, and these were distributed in strange fashion. The settlers simply helped themselves. The postmaster couldn't read the names on the envelopes!

After Washington Territory was established, Simmons became Indian agent under Governor Isaac I. Stevens. He arranged treaties with the various tribes of western Washington, and presumably both he and the Indian chief made their X's at the bottom when a treaty had been reduced to writing.

The stubbornness the man from Kentucky had displayed at his first meeting with Dr. McLoughlin was exhibited later on as well. The treaty of 1846, settling the boundary question between Canada and the United States, provided that the property rights of the Hudson's Bay Company and its subsidiary, the Puget Sound Agricultural Company, were to be respected. Before final payment was made, Dr. Tolmie tried to expand the companies' holdings by driving a herd of wild cattle across the Nisqually River to establish a beachhead on the south shore. This caused one of Washington's first public meetings to be held—at Tumwater, November 5, 1848. Mike Simmons called the meeting to order. The irate settlers gave Tolmie one week in which to return the cattle to the north side of the stream, and he complied.

When American rule over the region north of the Columbia had been established by treaty, the settlers there transferred their irritations from the Hudson's Bay Company to the settlers south of the Columbia. The distances the northern Oregonians, especially those on the sound, had to travel to do business with the territorial government at Oregon City and later at Salem were costly in time and money. Some of the settlers felt, too, that the Willamette Valley people, who were in the majority, were little interested in the welfare of the northerners.

At the Fourth of July celebration in Olympia in 1851, John B. Chapman started a movement to establish a separate territory for what was then generally called Northern Oregon. He referred, in the course of his oration, to the "future state of Columbia," and the reference was so enthusiastically received that an adjourned meeting was held at which a call was issued for a convention at Cowlitz on August 29. Michael Simmons was one of the delegates to the two-day session at Cowlitz. He was appointed, with John B. Chapman and Francis S. Balch, on a committee to prepare a memorial asking for separate territorial status.

Another committee recommended the creation of four new counties, one to be called Simmons. But even though the

Oregon territorial legislature granted the request in regard to only this one county, Mike Simmons declined the honor. Instead it was named Thurston County for Oregon's first delegate to Congress, Samuel R. Thurston, who put through the Donation Land Claim Act.

The founder of Tumwater was present at Monticello, present-day Longview, on November 25, 1852, when the next convention was held to act on the recommendations of the committee to which he had been named. The convention called for establishment of the Territory of Columbia. This was a rather brash request from such a small group of people; the population of the part of Oregon territory north of the Columbia was only about two thousand. However, the Oregon legislature agreed to the proposal; its members perhaps did not want to be bothered with the few Americans living so far away from Salem. Joseph Lane, then delegate to Congress, submitted the two memorials, and the following March, Congress established the separate territory. The speed with which this happened was in sharp contrast to the delay the memorials of the original Oregon Country had encountered.

Congress adopted only one significant amendment. It changed the proposed name from Columbia to Washington, in honor of the first President.

Michael Simmons, having played an important role in the establishment of the first government of what was to become a state in 1889, twenty-two years after his death, retired to the forest on the south shore of Skookum Bay, half way from its mouth to the present town of Shelton. There he lived when Harvey W. Scott, long-time editor of the *Portland Oregonian*, knew him during Scott's boyhood.

Scott said in a speech at Olympia at the semicentennial celebration of Washington Territory on March 3, 1903:

Simmons was the leading man, the most important man in our part of the country. He was Indian agent and had great influence over the natives. His wife was a woman of gentle nature, yet of great force of character. She had many children, but kept open house the year around, where everybody was welcome. Her influence over the Indians, large bodies of whom were always encamped near her house, was remarkable.

Scott recalled particularly a "logroll" held at the Simmons' place on Skookum Bay in the summer of 1855.

"All the neighbors within a dozen miles were present—about thirty men and big boys—and most of the women and girls of the settlement came along for the social gathering and to help with the cookery. Oh, the glory and memory of that day!"

Mike Simmons should have let a county be named for him. No other Washingtonian deserved the honor more.

5 · TABITHA BROWN—
SMALL PACKAGE OF GUMPTION

Courage and stamina usually came in large sizes on the western frontier. Young men in their twenties or early thirties often stood six feet tall or higher and were built in proportion, with wide shoulders and lean bodies. A splendid physique was a valuable asset when one was called upon to go days without food or water, to wade in icy beaver ponds or to fight Indians.

There were some exceptions to this rule, notably Kit Carson, who was a little fellow.

Another exception was neither young nor large, nor even masculine. She didn't fight Indians and she didn't trap beaver, but she survived ordeals of the trail equal in severity to those which mountain men considered horrible enough to write home about. And after that she still had enough grit and gumption left to make her own distinct mark on the Oregon Country.

The little, old lady was Tabitha Brown, who was sixty-six years old when she crossed the plains in 1846. She was about five feet tall and weighed no more than 108 pounds—after she had been eating regularly for a couple of years in Oregon. One leg was lame from paralysis, and she walked with a cane. She was indisputable proof that courage and stamina sometimes come in very small packages indeed.

Grandma Brown's life had been a strange mixture of erudition and adventure ever since she married Clark Brown, an Episcopal clergyman, at Brimfield, Massachusetts, on December 1, 1799. Tabitha Moffett was her maiden name, and her father was a physician. She was nineteen when she became the bride of the Reverend Mr. Brown. Captain John Brown, her husband's brother, provided the adventure. He also became a cause of deep concern to her in her late years.

John Brown was a sea captain, as were so many other New Englanders of that era. He sailed to distant lands and came home at infrequent intervals with stirring tales of storms and wrecks and run-ins with pirates. Once he was captured by the French during a period when France and the United States were on unfriendly terms. Long, long afterward his heirs were trying to recover damages for his losses in that adventure.

A bachelor, Captain John made his home with his brother and Tabitha whenever he was in home port. Tabitha's sons, Orus and Manthano, were delighted with the stories their uncle told. Tabitha's daughter, Pherne, undoubtedly enjoyed them, too, for many years later she was as eager as anybody to set out for Oregon, a journey that rivaled in daring the voyages made by the sea rovers of Massachusetts.

The Reverend Mr. Brown died in 1817 in Maryland, where he had accepted a pastorate. Soon after that, Orus and Manthano persuaded their mother to buy a sloop, with which, like their uncle, they meant to find adventure and make their fortune.

They were shipwrecked, instead, off the New England coast, and Tabitha cast about for some safer but still rewarding life for her boys. The Missouri frontier, halfway between the oceans, appeared to be just such a place, and in 1824 the family moved to St. Charles near St. Louis. Tabitha had been teaching school in Maryland and Virginia since her husband's death, and she continued to teach the settlers' children at St. Charles.

Captain John, in his middle fifties by now, quit the sea and went with Tabitha and the children to Missouri. He bought a house in St. Charles, and Pherne and her husband, Virgil Pringle, made their home with him. Tabitha herself preferred to be independent of her children and had a place of her own.

Missouri was the starting place for Oregon. Exciting accounts of the distant land by the Pacific Ocean drifted back along the trail when the westward migration quickened in the 1840s. Captain Brown must have sniffed the sea in these stories, and Tabitha, too, undoubtedly felt the urge to move on.

Finally in 1843, the year of the "Great Migration" to Oregon, Orus yielded to the stories of the West. He and several others joined the wagon trains that were straggling out across Kansas and Nebraska in the first major surge of American settlers. He spent a year on the Tualatin Plains where Joe Meek and several other mountain men were living—to "test the soil." In 1845 he returned.

"I've found paradise!" the forty-five-year-old adventurer exclaimed as the family gathered around to hear about his travels. He persuaded his mother, sister and uncle to sell their property and prepare to start for Oregon early in 1846. Evidently they didn't need much urging. But brother Manthano wasn't well, and his wife didn't wish to leave her family. So he remained on his farm near Kansas City.

On April 15, 1846, the sixty-six-year-old Grandma Brown, Captain John, now seventy-seven, Orus and his wife and eight children and the Pringles and their five children started out in a train of wagons from St. Charles. Tabitha had provided herself with a good ox-wagon team and supplies and equipment for the comfort of herself, Captain Brown and her driver. It was a fine outfit the little, old lady had obtained for the trip. The wagon had a carpet on the floor and was furnished with a bed, a mirror, a water barrel, a bookcase and Tabitha's favorite rocking chair. It was almost as comfortable as the house trailers tourists nowadays pull behind their cars.

During the day, Tabitha sat on the seat with her driver. Captain John rode horseback and camped with the other unattached men at night. Grandma prepared his meals, and in the evenings after supper she sat by her wagon in her rocker, cane by her side, entertaining her grandchildren and the other youngsters of the train while their mothers attended to their everlasting chores.

The journey was a pleasant one for some fourteen hundred miles, all the way across the Great Plains and the Rockies to Fort Hall, in present-day Idaho. Then, with only six hundred miles left, the usual route went along the Snake River to the Columbia and down that stream to the Willamette Valley. But a large number of the immigrants were persuaded to take a newly discovered short-cut as a much quicker way to the valley.

Orus Brown, having been over the old trail before, acted as a pilot for some of the immigrants. He had already started out for the Columbia before the southern route promoters appeared. Nevertheless the Pringles, Tabitha and Captain John, along with many others, decided to take the short-cut without asking Orus' advice.

Though the southern route would be traveled later in comparative ease, the first wagon tracks were made with great difficulty. Tabitha's party discovered there were sixty miles of desert to cross without grass or water, and there were mountains to climb. Cattle gave out, wagons broke, and many immigrants took sick, some dying. They had to be constantly on guard against hostile Indians.

The trip from Fort Hall began in August. September passed, and with October came winterlike weather. Yet the travelers were still far from the Willamette. The Klamath and Rogue

River Indians attacked and stole nearly all the cattle. As the immigrants attempted passage through a precipitous canyon in the Umpqua Mountains, all of their wagons but one were broken. Grandma Brown lost hers, along with her comfortable bed, the water barrel and her rocking chair. All she had left was a horse that she was now compelled to ride.

"Our families were the first that started through the canyon, so that we got through the mud and rocks much better than those that followed," she later noted. The canyon was strewn with dead cattle, broken wagons, beds, clothing and everything but provisions, of which few remained. Passage through the canyon, which was only twelve miles long, required two or three weeks for some of the immigrants. Some died without warning, from fatigue and starvation. Others ate the flesh of cattle lying dead by the wayside.

Mud and water up to the horses' bellies made the passage a nightmare. At the end of this ordeal lay the beautiful Umpqua Valley, but it was inhabited only by Indians and wild beasts, and the Calapooya Mountains had yet to be crossed in mud, snow, hail and rain.

Virgil and Pherne Pringle and Tabitha held a family council there by the Umpqua. Captain John was too exhausted to participate. The word had been passed that everyone who could should "fly from starvation."

"You and Uncle John must go ahead, Mother, to save your lives!" declared Pherne, and her husband agreed. "We must stay here a few days to recruit our cattle."

Tabitha demurred but finally gave in to their wishes. The provisions were almost gone; only a little bacon and tea remained. Captain John would not long survive unless food for him was found.

Next morning, Virgil saddled Tabitha's and John's horses. The bacon was divided equally among the many hungry members of the family. Tabitha recalled that her share was three slices of bacon together with a cup of tea. There was no bread. The Pringles boosted the aged captain and his only slightly younger sister-in-law to the backs of their horses, and the old couple set out, hoping to overtake five wagons that had left camp the day before and not knowing whether they would ever see their family again.

Tabitha rode in the lead. The feeble old man followed, slumped in his saddle. About sunset they caught up with two of the families that had left earlier. However, their cattle had given out, and they had no food. Tabitha and John camped with the other travelers that night in an oak grove without any supper. Next morning the elderly pilgrims rode off again, alone, hoping they would find the three other wagons and some food.

Though concerned about her own and her companion's safety and though suffering from hunger and fatigue, Grandma Brown was alert to her surroundings. She remarked the beauty of the mountains and valleys through which they passed— and her sharp eyes picked out the figures of two Indians in the distance.

By afternoon, Captain John was falling farther behind. He complained that he had a "swimming in the head and a pain in his stomach." Two or three hours later he became delirious and fell from his horse.

Tabitha was in a predicament. She was afraid to alight from her own horse because it was not accustomed to women riders and might run away. Besides, how would a slight, lame woman get back in the saddle again? The old man tried to rise to his feet but couldn't.

Fortunately, Grandma had the captain's *lignum vitae* cane with her, as well as her own. Riding close to the fallen man she stuck his cane in the ground near him. Following her instructions, he grasped the cane and pulled himself upright.

"Walk!" ordered Tabitha.

Captain John tried to do so. He tottered along a little way, then collapsed again. At that point a person of less character might well have given up, but not Grandma! She noticed a slight depression in the ground close by her fallen brother-in-law. She led his horse there and persuaded John to crawl over and grasp the stirrup. Tugging with all her might, Tabitha finally got her companion seated on his horse.

"Hold fast to the mane and I'll lead your horse by its bridle," the determined old lady commanded. The old man hung on.

For two miles they proceeded in this manner. Then they came to another mountain. Even a woman with the gumption of a mountain man could not lead another horse over such an obstacle. But by now Captain John had recovered sufficiently to manage for himself. They crossed the mountain safely and came into a large valley. Scanning the wide, solitary expanse hopefully, Tabitha was disappointed again. There wasn't a wagon in sight, but tracks were visible.

She followed them across the plain until the sun sank so low she could no longer see. Rain was slanting against the mountains in the distance. Grandma Brown had come to the end of her day.

She climbed down from her horse, careful not to frighten it. She tied the animal to a tree with a rope and removed her saddle and saddlebags. She had carried a wagon sheet under the saddle, and she flung this over the limb of a tree. It made a "fine tent."

John, still slumped in his saddle, watched Tabitha's activity with a bemused air.

"What are you going to do?" he asked finally.

"I'm going to camp for the night," replied the old lady.

The captain's head sank lower. With a groan he fell to the ground.

Prudent as always, Tabitha first made sure of the captain's horse, tying it also to a tree. Then she stripped it of saddle and blankets which she placed in her rude tent. Now she was ready for the captain. Helping him up, she fairly carried him on her frail back to the shelter. He was almost unconscious as she laid him on the ground and covered him with blankets. Tabitha seated herself cross-legged behind him. She did not think he would live through the night.

No one could state the situation better than Grandma Brown later did herself:

"Pause for a moment and consider the situation. Worse than alone, in a savage wilderness, without food, without fire, cold and shivering, wolves fighting and howling all around me. Dark clouds hid the stars. All as solitary as death. But that same kind Providence that I had always known was watching over me still. I committed all to Him and felt no fear. . . ."

Tabitha's faith was well placed. The night's rest restored the captian enough so that he could stand on his own feet. At sunrise, Tabitha roused him, pulled down the tent and saddled the horses. And while she was planning how to get John and herself back on the horses, one of the immigrants they had been following showed up, as if in answer to her prayers. The man was hunting deer and had managed to shoot one. Half a mile ahead was his wagon and the others Tabitha had been following. In a little while, the two old people were filling their shrunken stomachs with fresh meat.

Not only had Providence spared the elderly travelers from starvation, but also from possible death at the hands of savages. Fresh tracks of two Indians were noted by Tabitha and her rescuer within a few feet of where she had made the shelter. Later they learned that a Mr. Newton had been robbed and slain by Indians only a short distance away, though his wife's life was spared because she was a woman.

Soon a reunion with their family added to the joy of the old ones' deliverance. While they and their new companions were crossing the valley toward the Calapooyas, the Pringles caught up with them. The family was overjoyed to be together again and to learn that none of them had succumbed to the vicissitudes of the wilderness. The Pringles had been near starvation after Tabitha and Uncle John left them. Virgil had tried to shoot a wolf for food, but had been too weak to hold his rifle steady. Then a son, who had gone hunting, returned with some game and they ate again, their food salted with tears of thankfulness.

The Calapooyas proved to be extremely difficult to cross. The mountains were covered with snow, and a road had to be cut through the timber. The wagons could cover only a mile or two a day, and, thus, many days were required to reach the northern side.

Again the provisions ran low. So Virgil Pringle set off on horseback for the settlements. He didn't know how long he would be gone or if, indeed, he could even get through.

In a week or so the family's food was all gone. Pherne and the children wept over their precarious position, but not Tabitha! The old lady was convinced that tears would bring no solution. She was proud that through all her sufferings in crossing the plains, she had not once sought relief by the shedding of tears, nor thought the family should not live to reach the settlements. Now she reaffirmed her faith in Providence.

Clark, the eldest Pringle boy, shot one of his father's best working oxen so that the family might eat. It had no fat on it and the meat on the bones was stringy. But at least this staved off starvation.

One night, as Tabitha, John, Pherne and the children lay in their tents, trying to forget their troubles until morning, they heard horses approaching. Then came shouts of "Halloo!" and the old woman knew that the Providence she trusted so implicitly had justified her faith once again. In the shouts she recognized not only the voice of her son-in-law Virgil but also that of her son Orus.

Orus had arrived in the settlements in September by the old Columbia River route. He became extremely concerned about his family when they did not arrive within a reasonable period. Then news reached him that immigrants were in trouble in southern Oregon, so he set out with four pack animals carrying provisions for their relief.

Now that Orus and Virgil were back with the family, directing renewed efforts to get out of the mountains, the little group began to move again. Five miles from camp they met a party of French-Indian travelers with packhorses. They hired six of the animals and made their way slowly toward civilization, rationing their food. On Christmas Day they reached Salem and at two o'clock that afternoon, Grandma walked into the house of a missionary. It was the first house she had set foot in for nine long months.

One can see Tabitha looking over the missionary's house with a critical eye. It did not meet her housekeeping standards.

"His wife was as ignorant and useless as a heathen goddess," confided the old lady later.

The upshot was that, though tired from the long trip and the ordeals she had just overcome, the slightly built, elderly immigrant found a job for the winter. The missionary asked her to take charge of his house and family. This she did, earning board for herself and Captain John by performing household duties.

She needed some cash, too, but she had none—except one small coin. During the last few days of her travels down the Willamette she had felt something in one of the fingers of her glove. At first she thought it was a button, but when she turned the glove inside out to remove the object she was delighted to find a "picayune," a coin worth six and one-fourth cents.

With this as capital, she built her "fortune" to thirty dollars before spring arrived. First she bought three large needles. Then she traded off some of her old clothes to Indian squaws for buckskin. From this she made gloves for the men and women of the community.

When spring came, the elderly woman was on the move again. She accepted an invitation from missionaries to spend the summer at Clatsop Plains, just south of Astoria on the Pacific Ocean. It was a long journey by open boat from Salem to the sea, first down the Willamette and then down the Columbia to its mouth. But the youthful spirit in the old body reveled in the bracing ocean air.

Besides visiting, Grandma Brown bathed in the Pacific!

Picture the small former New Englander, who as a girl had played in the surf of the Atlantic, limping joyously into the cold breakers of the Pacific! Did she go in gradually, as many younger persons do, wetting only her toes at first? More than likely Tabitha Brown leaped in, holding up a modest garment by one hand and steadying herself with her cane by the other. "The surf of two oceans has rolled over me!" she exclaimed.

In October, Tabitha spent thirteen days in an open boat traveling from Astoria to Oregon City. There she was only twenty miles from Tualatin Plains where Orus and his family lived. It would not do for a mother to come so close to her son's house without dropping in for a visit, Tabitha told herself. So she gave a neighbor of Orus' two dollars to take her in his wagon to the plains. He had come to Oregon City with produce from his farm.

Independent as always, Tabitha planned to stay only two weeks with Orus and his family. However, he introduced her to the Reverend and Mrs. Harvey Clark, missionaries from New York, who invited her to spend the winter with them. The Clarks were about the age of her own children, the old lady noted, and they looked to her for advice!

Through Mr. Clark, Tabitha now found a new outlet for her housekeeping and teaching abilities. The migration of 1847 was hard hit by sickness. Many children were left motherless. The poor children arriving in the settlements without proper care were of great concern to Tabitha.

One day she said to Mr. Clark, "Why has Providence frowned on me and left me poor in this world? Had he blessed me with riches, as he has many others, I know right well what I would do."

"What would you do?" asked the missionary.

"I would establish myself in a comfortable house and receive all poor children and be a mother to them."

Assured that she was in earnest, Clark promised to help her achieve that laudable ambition.

The log meetinghouse at West Tualatin Plains, soon to be known as Forest Grove, was placed at Grandma Brown's disposal. There she started a school, open to rich and poor alike. Parents who could paid one dollar a week for board and tuition. Tabitha planned to work a year for nothing, and Mr. Clark and other settlers helped with provisions. Thus was born one of the first schools in the Oregon Country. Within a decade it was chartered as Pacific University and is a going concern to this day.

Neighbors collected whatever old knives, forks, dishes and

tin pans they could spare from their scant supplies, and the former teacher of Maryland, Virginia and Missouri was busy at her chosen profession again, though her efforts were expended more in housekeeping than in teaching. In the summer the settlers built her a boarding house and she soon had thirty boarders of both sexes from age four to twenty-one.

Grandma Brown also planted a garden from which she furnished vegetables for her boarders. Settlers provided beef. Consequently, the substantial dinners she served consisted of boiled beef and vegetables. Dessert, in season, was wild strawberries gathered by the girls in teacups on the surrounding prairie.

Tabitha saw to it that the meals were served properly. The table was covered with a white cloth. There were sugar bowls and saltcellars. Spoonholders were gay, made of cardboard covered with colorful calico.

The slight, lame mistress of the school was described by one scholar as delicate of face, with blue eyes and gray hair. In her manner of expression she was always young, a companion of the children, rather than a disciplinarian.

At dusk, she called them in from play. They took their seats and together repeated the evening prayer. In the mornings, especially on Sundays, Tabitha awakened the children with song. Her voice was still sweet and strong. She made the youngsters feel cheerful all week long.

And besides doing all the housekeeping work, Tabitha fashioned many of her own small conveniences. One was an oven built of a wooden framework covered with clay. When a fire was started in the oven the wooden frame burned away and the clay hardened like brick.

Cloth for the girls' dresses was obtained from the Hudson's Bay Company at Vancouver. The company would sell from only one bolt at a time. Usually this was a gaudy calico that appealed to the Indian women. Grandma Brown watched for an opportunity to buy a whole bolt of white muslin. The delighted girls of her school blossomed out all in white for a picnic.

In 1849, the fee was raised to two dollars a week, Tabitha to provide everything and to keep whatever was left. Two years later, a further increase to two-fifty was approved. That year Grandma Brown mixed with her own hands 3423 pounds of flour!

By 1855, Tabitha felt entitled to a rest. Her little boarding school had grown into a university. She wrote to relatives in the East about her accomplishments:

You must be judges whether I have been doing good or evil. I have labored for myself and the rising generation, but I have now quit hard work, and live at my ease, independent as to wordly concerns. I have a nicely furnished white frame house on a lot in town, within a short distance of the public buildings. That I rent for $100 a year. I have eight other lots, without buildings, worth $150 each. I have eight cows and a number of young cattle. The cows I rent out for their milk and one-half of their increase. I have rising $1,100 cash due me; $400 of it I have donated to the University, besides $100 I gave to the Academy three years ago. This much I have been able to accumulate by my own industry, independent of my children, since I drew 6¼ cents from the finger of my glove.

Release from an earlier responsibility enabled Grandma Brown to accomplish all this. Captain Brown lived only a little more than a year after he and his sister-in-law arrived at Salem. He died there February 19, 1848. But in that year he too was not inactive. He met an old friend of his sailing days, Captain Stark, and accepted the latter's invitation to journey to San Francisco. He returned "very fleshy" and short of breath, but wearing new clothes and bringing "extravagant presents" for the family, just as he had done so many years before in Massachusetts.

Tabitha outlived the captain by ten years. She died in Salem May 4, 1858, just three days past her seventy-eighth birthday.

A memorial of petrified wood was later raised at Pacific University. The symbolism was perfect. Petrified wood is very old. Ordinarily a soft material, wood in this form is as sturdy as rock. The little, old lady for whom the memorial was erected was rocklike in fortitude and faith, yet retained the grain of kindness and gentleness that ennobles her sex.

6 · HENRY YESLER —
STEAM AND A SKIDROAD

If the men of Seattle had been looking seaward on a certain gray day in October, 1852, they would have seen a dugout canoe rounding Duwamish Head from the direction of Alki Point. It dipped and rose in the whitecaps of the open water of Puget Sound, then settled into a smooth glide as it reached the protection of Elliott Bay. Seated in the well-shaped vessel, which a native craftsman had fashioned by fire and chisel from a cedar log, was a stocky, ruddy-faced man in his early forties.

However, the men of Seattle were not looking. They were too busy. The five of them, the entire adult male population of the community, were making the forest ring with the sound of sharp blade biting into solid wood.

They had rolled off their wall-shelf beds in their tiny log cabins at cheerless dawn. Shouldering axes and adzes, they had picked their way through the dense forest to the sag (a dip in the high bluff) for another long day of felling trees and squaring logs into timber. Mist obscured the snowclad peaks of the Olympics across the sound. The water, reflecting the overcast, was the dreary color of slate.

The future of Seattle, freshly named for an Indian chief, did not appear bright that morning. The "city," which a few weeks before had been tentatively laid out, appeared now as ephemeral as the wisps of mist. In the cold reality of morning, Seattle was only a forest with a handful of cabins.

The canoe on the bay glided closer to the sag, but the men of Seattle didn't see it. The tempo of their chopping picked up as their stiff muscles unlimbered with their effort. After a bit, another timber was ready to wrestle into the water, a job that took brute strength even here where the land was level with the sound. Soon a little sailing vessel would arrive from San Francisco, and they would have enough timbers to trade for a winter's supply of flour, salt pork, butter and sugar. With these and the game, fish and clams, plentiful in the sound, their families would fare rather well.

But, man, this was a hard way to make timbers! If only they had a sawmill!

The canoe pulled up on the beach and its occupant stepped out. He made his way through the underbrush toward the place where the forest rang. The men did not see or hear him until he was in their midst.

He was a man of obvious means, more mature than the woodchoppers; the stranger's clothes indicated prosperity. His trim beard and his air of assurance added to his appearance of well-being.

The men laid down their tools and greeted the stranger, who came right to the point.

"I'm Henry Yesler," he said. "I'm looking for a place to build a sawmill."

One would like to think that the mist lifted at that moment and that the sun peeped through, changing the slate-colored sound into brilliant blue. Here, in person, was the answer to their prayers. Here was a man who could ease their labors. Here was a man who obviously had money enough to start an industry that would provide jobs and attract more settlers, who in turn would buy lots for stores and factories and homes. Seattle some day might be as large as New York! This was their dream—a dream so real that the place first settled in these parts, over there across the bay, had actually been named New York. On second thought, the settlers had added the word "Alki" which was Chinook jargon for "by and by." New York–Alki, they called the one-cabin city.

The men gathered around Mr. Yesler and shook his hand. They introduced themselves: Arthur Denny, William Bell, Carson Boren, Dr. David Maynard and David Denny.

It was some time before the excited settlers learned what kind of mill Mr. Yesler had in mind. Any sort was better than none, even a muley run by water power such as Mike Simmons had erected at Tumwater.

But Mr. Yesler had bigger ideas. He intended to build a *steam mill* like the one installed two years before in Portland. It took real power to cut these big trees into lumber, and that required steam! Water wheels, like those at Oregon City, Fort Vancouver and Tumwater, couldn't meet California's great demand for boards and timbers.

Arthur Denny invited Mr. Yesler to his house for dinner. Mary Denny did her best to convert her meager supplies into an appetizing meal. And then they talked, for hours, about happenings in the States and in Oregon and about Yesler and his plans.

The newcomer, it turned out, was a native of Maryland where he had learned the trade of carpenter and millwright. He had gone to Massillon, Ohio, in 1830 as a young man of twenty. There he had engaged in the sawmill business until 1851 when he went west to Oregon with the intention of expanding his lumber interests. He worked at his trade in Portland for a time, then went to California where he operated a mine near Marysville. But mining wasn't for him. He was after all a sawmill man. Then a ship captain, who had been trading in Puget Sound, told him of the wonderfully tall trees and deep water here. So, here he was now, ready to build if he could find a place that suited him.

Yes, he was married, he told Mrs. Denny. His wife's name

was Sarah. She'd join him on the sound if he decided to stay.

When Henry Yesler talked or cogitated, his hands were seldom still. Sometimes he tugged at his longish nose, but usually he whittled. With a sharp pocket knife he put points on twigs. If a piece of soft wood was handy, he would fashion it into novel shapes. In the next few hours he whittled a great deal.

Yesler allowed that he liked Seattle. The people appeared friendly and full of ambition.

"Yes, and the water is deep clear up to shore," put in one of the settlers. This was the reason the group had moved here from New York–Alki, he explained. The previous February, Arthur Denny, Bell and Boren had taken a clothesline and a bundle of horseshoes and paddled over from Alki. Tying the line on the horseshoes, they had sounded all along the bay shore. They could hardly touch bottom. This was a wonderful harbor, whereas Alki Point was exposed to the storms of the sound and its water was too shallow.

The prospective mill operator agreed with all this, but said that the only logical site for a mill—on the little point at the sag—was already taken. Doc Maynard had a fish salting stand there and his little store. Yes, he liked the place fine, Mr. Yesler repeated; but he had been by Alki and Duwamish Head across the bay, and he guessed he would go back there and see what he could find.

The men of Seattle would not let opportunity slip through their fingers. While Mr. Yesler whittled another piece of wood, they huddled in earnest discussion. They had already shifted their original claims to make room for Doc Maynard's salmon salting business, one of them pointed out. They could shift once again to make room for a far more promising industry.

So Doc Maynard gave up his level place by the water, plus

a strip one hundred twenty feet wide along the north side of his claim. Boren offered a strip three hundred feet wide along the south edge of his claim, adjoining Maynard's. Maynard and Boren then compensated themselves by extending their claims eastward toward Lake Washington. As a result Yesler was offered a mill site on the sound and a shovel-shaped claim of three hundred twenty acres extending back up what is now known as Capitol Hill. The strip was the handle of the shovel, and the blade was a heavily forested fan-shaped extension on the hill.

The industrialist didn't tug his nose very long. It was a good offer. When the trees had been cut near the water and on the claims to the north, the strip would permit him to build a skidroad to his mill from the hill timber. With oxen dragging logs over the skidroad, he would have plenty of raw material for years to come.

But the settlers did more than furnish a site for new industry. They helped provide the buildings, too. Alongside the place where the mill was to rise, they erected a log cookhouse, larger than their own cabins. Then, while Yesler went off to San Francisco to buy machinery for his mill, they built a shed of rude planks to house the boiler and the saw.

One can imagine Denny, Maynard and the others standing back to look with pride on their handiwork. Here was Progress, with a capital "P." The *Columbian,* the weekly paper published at Olympia, fairly made them burst with enthusiasm when it ran an item on the mill that same month. It was the first time Seattle had been mentioned by name on a printed page.

Seattle's first press agent, undoubtedly Doc Maynard, was a little overly enthusiastic when he told the editor the mill would be in operation by November. But by the following March it was whining its way through the first of the great trees that grew all around it. Every man in town got a job working in the mill or logging for it.

By present-day standards Yesler's mill wasn't much of a plant. It would hardly rate classification as a "peckerwood," today's nickname for a small operation. It cut only fourteen thousand feet a day. But, since almost all the work except the actual sawing was done by hand, it was a boon to the penniless settlers.

The mill furnished boards for houses, as well, and soon dwellings built of lumber, rather than of logs, began springing up. This appearance of civilization, together with logging and sawmilling jobs, drew more and more settlers and tradesmen. Besides providing work and lumber, Yesler was liberal with his money. He lent cash to his neighbors, often without security, and not infrequently at a loss.

Indeed Seattle's first capitalist was wealthy only by comparison with the first group of settlers. For a long time he couldn't even afford to buy a whistle. A circular saw, hung by the cookhouse door, called the workers to duty and to chow. When Yesler pounded on it, every Indian in his hut and every pioneer in his cabin was aroused. This improvised gong and the whistle which eventually replaced it made sweet music. The community awoke by this pleasant sound of industry, ate by it and went to bed by it. Many years passed before anyone complained of the 5:00 A.M. whistle.

Sawdust from the mill, hauled away from the saw by wheelbarrow, soon covered the mud flats at the sag. A fire burned continuously near the mill, fed by the slabs the whining saw sliced from the outsides of the logs. These, too, the settlers found pleasant. They didn't think of the pall of smoke as air pollution but as money in the bank. Besides, the fragrance of newly sawed lumber is a splendid deodorizer.

Yesler built a little white house near the mill for his wife

Sarah. They lived there for thirty years.

The principal demand for lumber didn't come from Henry's struggling neighbors at first. San Francisco was the main market. The Gold Rush created a need for mine timbers, lumber for houses and planks for wharves. The growing city by the Golden Gate suffered recurrently from fire. It was constantly rebuilding. This made business for Henry Yesler and other mills that soon sprang up in neighboring communities, as well as for those already operating in Oregon.

Twenty sailing vessels shuttled between Seattle and San Francisco that first summer. Sometimes a ship was forced to lie at anchor for several days while the busy little mill sawed enough boards to make a cargo. The editor of the *Columbian* had been right. Mr. Yesler's mill was as good as a gold mine, though he was to find his real bonanza in the growth of the city. This made his claim and those of his neighbors worth hundreds of thousands. "Alki," the "by and by" of the Chinook jargon, became "now" during the lifetimes of most of those early settlers.

The great demand for lumber put everyone not engaged at the mill to logging, even the farmers who had settled on the Duwamish. Since the first oxen were not brought to Seattle until 1854, every operation the first year had to be performed by human effort.

The bluff which rose steeply from the bay was covered with huge trees. They grew so thickly that a man could get lost among them, as Dr. Henry A. Smith actually did. His experience became a classic joke at the cookhouse where Yesler and his crew used to relax from their hard labor.

It seems that Smith had settled on a cove north of the other claims. At first he came to the village by canoe, but after a few months he decided to blaze a trail through the forest so he could travel by land. After pushing through the timber for an hour or two he came to a clearing. Looking about, he was struck by the similarity of this clearing to his own. The cabin looked like his and a rooster on a nearby stump was a dead-ringer for his own. Soon a woman came out of the cabin. Her figure and clothing seemed familiar, too. Suddenly, Dr. Smith realized that the woman was his mother. He had walked in a circle in the deep, dark forest.

The density of the timber also assured the mill of a more than adequate supply of raw material. Even so, transportation was not easy. To get the logs from the bluff to the mill, the men rolled or slid them to the water with the help of cant hooks. Then they towed them with light skiffs to the sag. Their only power was their own arms pulling on the oars. The work was always hard and sometimes dangerous.

John Holgate was a great one for keeping a diary. One day Yesler found Holgate's diary on the ground where the settler had dropped it. The last entry read: "Started for Yesler's mill. Fell off into the water."

The genial mill owner added "and drowned" before returning the diary with a straight face to its owner. One can imagine the guffaws this brought forth at the cookhouse when Yesler told about it.

For many years the log cookhouse was Seattle's community center. Primarily it was a mess hall for workingmen, but in the early days everyone was a workingman. The first religious service was held there by Catholic Bishop Modeste Demers, who stopped by on his way to Victoria. It was the city's first tavern, first of many that were to line the shovel-handle of Yesler's claim as it progressed from trail, to skidroad, to a street known as Yesler Way. Everyone was welcome, whether or not he could pay for his food or for a place to unroll his blankets. In addition to the purely social gatherings there the justice of the peace held court in one corner and the commissioners of King County met with Henry Yesler, county auditor.

In 1854 two Indians were convicted of the murder of a white man named McCormick, crewman on a lumber schooner. The trial was held in the cookhouse. The community's first lynching followed. It, too, started in the cookhouse, being planned there by hotheaded settlers and sailors from a vessel then in the bay. The sailors furnished block and tackle from their ship. Then, along with the violent settlers, they broke into a cabin where the Indians were being held and hanged them to a tree near Yesler's mill. At a later trial the ringleaders of the "necktie party" were acquitted. Trouble that had been brewing for some time with the Indians was thus brought to a head.

The Sound Indians were usually peaceable, but more aggressive tribesmen from east of the Cascades egged them on to make a stand against the white man's intrusion. It was their last chance, now that their backs were to the Pacific. Dissatisfaction was strong among the Indians because of treaties that Isaac I. Stevens, first territorial governor, had induced them to sign. The result was the Seattle Indian "war" of 1855–56.

During this terrifying crisis Yesler played a major part in saving the settlement. He had employed Indians as well as white men in his mill and had treated them well. They considered him a friend. Salmon Bay Curley was particularly friendly toward the mill operator. From time to time Henry gave Curley small quantities of ammunition and tobacco. These the Indian in turn traded to unfriendly Indians, who had already murdered some settlers on the Duwamish, in exchange for information.

By January 25, 1856, one thousand Klickitats from east of the mountains had been ferried across Lake Washington by Sound Indians. They were advancing through the woods toward the settlement. Curley and another friendly native,

Indian Jim, managed to sit in on a council of war held that evening by hostile chiefs. The first plan was to attack the settlers at two o'clock in the morning. But Indian Jim pointed out that marines from the sloop-of-war *Decatur,* which had been standing off the shore for some days, were on guard duty in the settlement at that hour. A better time to attack, he argued, was at the end of the night watch when the marines had gone back aboard the *Decatur* for breakfast, leaving the settlement unguarded. Curley then pleaded that Henry Yesler's life be spared, because he had given the Indians work in his mill, but the hostile chiefs asserted that all whites must die.

The plan almost succeeded. The marines, as Indian Jim had foretold, went aboard the warship at daybreak. The hostile Indians crept to the edge of the forest poised for the attack. But somehow Indian Jim managed to elude them and brought word to the settlement of the impending disaster.

Yesler was notified at once; he paddled hurriedly out to the *Decatur* where the marines were just sitting down to breakfast. They were sent ashore again, their hunger unappeased.

A howitzer, set up on shore, was fired at the place where the Indians were believed to be congregated. The *Decatur*'s batteries raked the edge of the forest, and the marines and volunteers exchanged volleys with the concealed natives. Settlers, including women and children, ran in panic to a recently built blockhouse while this shooting was going on. All made it safely. That night the Indians retreated, burning outlying cabins as they went.

A return of the hostiles was expected, so the settlers prepared for a long siege. They decided to build a stockade around the whole town. Henry Yesler supplied the lumber for this elaborate defense. Two fences five feet high and a foot and a half apart were constructed of closely placed boards. The space between them was filled with sawdust. The settlers were sure their fort was bulletproof, but fortunately it was never tested. The Indians did not attack again.

The miller had, however, yet another part to play before the Indian danger could be considered ended. Because of his friendship with them, he served as an emissary to the tribesmen skulking in the woods east of Lake Washington. He paddled across the lake, found the war parties in their hiding places and persuaded them to give themselves up to be placed on reservations.

Though the city was saved, the "war" put a damper on its progress. Many newcomers departed, some to a new gold rush on the Fraser River in Canada. But the original settlers stayed on, still embued with their dream. Among those that stayed was Henry Yesler.

From the beginning, the people of Seattle realized that they must find some easy way of crossing the Cascade Mountains if they were to prosper. Puget Sound was as close to Wallula, where the pioneers reached the Columbia, as was the Willamette Valley. But a man could glide down the river more easily than he could climb over the mountains. Seattle had been hardly settled before the pioneers there began searching for a pass through the mountains along the Snoqualmie River.

Without money it was impossible to build and maintain a road. Finally, in 1867, the legislature appropriated $2000 for a Snoqualmie Pass road, provided King County raised a like amount. Henry Yesler was one of those soliciting funds. The money was raised, and a road, of sorts, was constructed over the mountains. So now for the first time Seattle had a direct tie with its hinterland. But, to be honest, this wasn't exactly the kind of road a city could depend upon for rapid growth. It was more like a trail.

The imaginative miller, stockier now in his sixties, whittled his woodbox full of shavings as he pondered the problem. His gray beard waggled with excitement when the answer came to him. Once again his mill would serve Seattle. His proposed solution was both magnanimous and sensational. In 1875 he sponsored the "First Grand Lottery of Washington Territory." First prize was to be his sawmill, "valued at $100,000"!

Handbills were printed and tickets sold. Some Washingtonians, however, were bitterly against gambling. They opposed a lottery even though its purpose was good. So they took Yesler to court, and the lottery was held to be unconstitutional. Another dream for Seattle supremacy was temporarily shattered.

Also discouraging to the struggling metropolis were its railroad setbacks. Even before Henry Yesler appeared on that October day in '52, the settlers were certain that within a few years Seattle would become the terminus of a transcontinental railroad. Their vision of a great city—"New York by and by"—included tracks spanning the continent and ending, of course, on Elliott Bay. David Denny named one of the first imaginary streets "Depot Street." Governor Stevens, on his way west to become first chief executive of the territory, surveyed a route across the continent for a northern railroad.

But the years went by without construction of such a road. In 1864, dreams were revived with news that the federal government had granted a charter to the Northern Pacific Railroad. In 1870 Jay Cooke, the eastern financier, began building the road—westward from Duluth—subsidized by a land grant covering sixty miles on each side of the right of way. But it was not yet to cross the mountains into Depot Street. Again the easy grade of the Columbia River interfered with Seattle's dream of a direct connection with the East. The railroad made a deal with the Oregon Steam Navigation Company to use the latter's tracks along the big river. Puget Sound would be served by a line running north from Kalama on the Columbia.

Yesler and the others were dismayed by this news, but they did not lose all hope. In their view, Seattle was the only logical terminus of this north-south route. Then, one day in 1873, came a shattering blow. The railroad builders had decided to skim the cream for themselves rather than let an already established community obtain the benefits that a railroad would bring. The terminus, they decided, would be at Commencement Bay. Men wept when the telegram containing this news arrived. Commencement Bay is twenty miles south of Seattle. The then little town of Tacoma had been started there only two years before. It had two hundred inhabitants to Seattle's two thousand. Now, however, the avarice of the railroad builders threatened to make it the metropolis of Puget Sound.

Seattle did not remain in shock very long. A few days later the citizens gathered at Yesler's Pavilion, which had replaced the now outgrown cookhouse. If the moguls would not build a railroad to their city, they decided to build one themselves! They would run it over the mountains to Walla Walla, so that the grain and other produce of eastern Washington would pour into Seattle instead of flowing down the Columbia to Portland. The people of Walla Walla were receptive to the idea, but they didn't raise any cash to help meet the estimated cost of the railroad (between three and four million dollars). The legislature didn't help either.

By spring of 1874 it was evident that Seattle would have to build its railroad without money. If each man would donate one day's work a week, it could be done, some said. So on May Day, the whole town turned out for a working picnic on the banks of the Duwamish. The women furnished the food, and the men brought their picks and shovels. But first there had to be speeches to start the project properly.

Henry Yesler stood by the wagon that served as a platform for the speakers. He was whittling as usual. Once in a while he tugged at his long nose above his gray beard. Finally, he was called on to say a few words. He threw away the stick on which he had been working, folded up his knife and climbed aboard the wagon. His words were few, indeed, as the *Intelligencer* made clear the next morning.

"It's time to quit fooling and go to work," he said. Then he and his companions spit on their hands and began to dig. But it took more than spit and ambition to lay steel clear across the territory.

The work continued for three years. It soon became evident that the road would never reach Walla Walla. It did reach coal deposits twelve miles away, however, and after a time Seattle coal became such an important commodity that the railroads had to come to the city, whether or not the eastern financiers favored the idea.

All was not struggle, however, during these years. The town had fun, too, and Henry Yesler helped furnish it, as he had from the start at the cookhouse. The mill owner enjoyed Fourth of July celebrations. One year he built a pavilion in his orchard for a community Independence Day shindig. He intended it to be only a temporary structure, but the people liked it so well that he decided to wall it in for permanent use. It became the new community center, more commodious and comfortable than the cookhouse. Christmas was just as big a day there as the Fourth of July. By 1864 the Yuletide celebration had become a regular event. A large fir tree was decorated with strings of popcorn and cranberries and lighted with homemade candles. Santa Claus handed out presents to the children, and he bore a strong resemblance to Henry L. Yesler.

In 1863, Seattle obtained its first newspaper, the *Gazette*. It was published from an office provided free by the mill owner. In 1865, Yesler and Charles Terry built the first water system. V-shaped flumes carried water to the town from springs in the hills. The flumes were built high enough above the ground so that wagons could pass under them. Henry later replaced the flumes with pipes made of logs through which holes had been bored by hand.

Sarah Yesler also participated in community affairs with her husband's good-natured encouragement. In 1871, feminist Susan B. Anthony spoke in one of the city's small churches. As a result of the meeting, the Female Suffrage Society was organized. One of its most active members was Mrs. Yesler. A man had to be mighty broad-minded to permit his wife to engage in such foolishness.

But Yesler could also be hard-nosed when that became necessary. In 1886, he was serving his second term as mayor. Thousands of Chinese who had helped build the railroads were now out of work. They flooded West Coast cities. White workmen became alarmed that the Chinese would drive down the wage scale by working for less money. The Americans began harassing the Chinese, burning their shanties and threatening their lives. In Seattle a mob herded several hundred Chinese to the docks and bought passage for them on a ship to San Francisco. Mayor Yesler took a strong stand for law and order, and the riots were put down with the help of state and federal troops.

In 1883, Henry built the finest house in Washington Territory, but Sarah Yesler did not enjoy it long. She died four years later. The house itself was nearly lost in June, 1889, when fire swept the city, destroying nearly every building on twenty-five city blocks and every mill and wharf in the central district. Yesler's house was saved by soaking hundreds of blankets in water and covering the roof and walls. He had sold his mill before the fire.

In his eightieth year, Henry remarried. But he and his new wife Minnie had only two years together. On December 15, 1892, Seattle's first outstanding industrialist died.

Henry Yesler is remembered not only for his contributions to Seattle and the Puget Sound country but also for an odd reason that would have made him and the boys chuckle down at the cookhouse if they had known about it.

A "skidroad" in the parlance of pioneer loggers was a path through the woods over which ox teams dragged, or skidded, logs to a mill or to a waterway. It was made by laying short logs crosswise. Over these the saw logs would slide more easily than if they were dragged through the mud to catch on protruding roots or rocks.

When Henry built his skidroad along the strip Maynard and Boren had given him, his only purpose was to haul logs. But in the process he unwittingly helped to coin an expression. For it was only natural that as Seattle grew, saloons, inexpensive lodginghouses, stores catering to workingmen's clothing and other accessories and places of questionable entertainment should spring up near the original tavern—the cookhouse. After a time, the skidroad, by now called "Yesler Way," was lined with such places. Loggers and millworkers from miles around came there to blow their stakes in a week or two of lusty living. It was natural that they should refer to the street and the area south of it, where additional honkytonks then stood, as the *Skidroad*.

Similar districts in other towns became known by the same term. Burnside Street in Portland and Pacific Avenue in Tacoma are counterparts of Yesler Way. They are the dividing lines between the "proper" and the somewhat rowdy parts of the cities. "Skidroad" is used correctly when applied to sections of western cities where honest woodsmen roomed and played in their robust way. One may be sure that Henry Yesler would have enjoyed his contribution to the American language.

Unfortunately, easterners who publish most of the nation's literature, have corrupted the word. They refer to the sleazy sections of all cities as "skid row," an expression absolutely without authentic origin or meaning. The only skidding these Bowerylike areas have ever known is the rapid downward slide of the human derelicts who exist there.

7 · CAPTAIN JOHN C. AINSWORTH—
RULER OF THE RIVERS

Christmas Day, 1850, dawned sunnily. There was a nip in the air, as there always is in winter when an east wind whips down the Columbia Gorge and sweeps away the moist, sea clouds. But at Milwaukie, a hamlet on the Willamette between well-established Oregon City and a stump town called Portland, few had time to shiver. Least of all Lot Whitcomb. The town proprietor, sawmill operator and postmaster was busier than anybody. For this day, his pride and joy, the first steamboat built on the Willamette, was to slide into the river to enhance both the fame of Mr. Whitcomb himself and that of his town, where he had property to sell.

The steamer was called the *Lot Whitcomb.* She was a handsome ship—one hundred sixty feet long and twenty-four feet wide and with a hold so deep a man could stand upright in it, if he wasn't over five feet, eight inches tall. Her side wheels were eighteen feet in diameter. Their housings rose clear above the hurricane deck to the texas.

Territorial Governor John P. Gaines looked her over carefully as she sat in her white beauty on the ways; he pronounced her excellent. So did the officers from Vancouver who had brought up the army's brass band for the occasion. Captain Frederick Morse of the schooner *Merchantman,* then loading lumber at Mr. Whitcomb's mill, cast his expert eye over the sleek vessel. She wasn't a sailer, but she looked real seaworthy, anyhow, he allowed.

Even Captain John C. Ainsworth liked her. He was an experienced steamboatman, who had taught Samuel L. Clemens

Sketch by famed Western artist Frederic Remington depicts a *Coureur de Bois*, French Canadian fur trapper. American mountain men also wore buckskin, though the cut of their clothes varied somewhat. Jedediah Smith, unlike most of the others, was smooth shaven. (*Oregon Historical Society*)

(LEFT) This painting at Whitman College, Walla Walla, Wash., shows Narcissa Whitman as a glamorous young woman. (*Whitman College*) (BELOW) Canadian artist Paul Kane visited the Whitman mission shortly before the massacre and sketched Tomahas, the Cayuse brave who murdered Dr. Marcus Whitman. (*Oregon Historical Society*)

A mural in the Oregon State Capitol rotunda shows Dr. John Mc-Loughlin welcoming Narcissa Whitman and Eliza Spalding to Vancouver in 1836. They were the first American women to cross the plains and mountains to the Oregon Country. (*Oregon State Highway Department Photo*)

The Whitman mission at Waiilatpu as it appeared in 1843. (*Oregon Historical Society*)

The meeting at Champoeg in 1843 when Joe Meek, former mountain man, rallied settlers to vote for a provisional government looking toward affiliation with the United States, rather than with Great Britain. Tradition has it that the United States won by two votes. Photo is of a mural in the Oregon State Capitol. (*Oregon State Highway Department Photo*)

Joe Meek, first United States marshal of Oregon Territory, which
covered the whole Pacific Northwest. He is wearing the brass-buttoned
coat in which he returned from Washington, D.C., after going there
as self-styled "Envoy Extraordinary and Minister Plenipotentiary."
He still wears his fur cap. (*Oregon Historical Society*)

Michael T. Simmons who led the first settlers to Puget Sound, against the wishes and advice of Dr. John McLoughlin. (*Oregon Historical Society*)

(ABOVE) Settlements grew rapidly in the Northwest wilderness. Main Street in Olympia, Washington, was lined solidly with houses and business build-

ings in 1870, barely 25 years after Michael Simmons and his companions established the first settlement at nearby Tumwater. (LEFT) Sketch of log structure in which Tabitha Brown started her school at present-day Forest Grove. (BELOW) Educational institutions grew as quickly as the towns. This old wood cut of Pacific University shows how Grandma Brown's little boarding school had developed into a respectable campus by 1870, or in less than 25 years. (*All Oregon Historical Society*)

(ABOVE) Typical Northwest skidroad over which giant logs were skidded to mill or waterway over smaller logs laid crosswise. Oxen provided the motive power. Such a skidroad built by Henry Yesler became a Seattle street and originated the term applied to workingmen's sections of western cities. (RIGHT) Henry Yesler, pictured here in later life, was Seattle's first industrialist and played a big part in the growth of the Northwest's largest city. (*Both Oregon Historical Society*)

(LEFT) Abigail Scott Duniway (seated) achieved final success in a forty-year campaign to give Northwest women the vote when on November 30, 1912, she wrote the official proclamation opening the polls to Oregon women. Governor Oswald West (right) asked Mrs. Duniway to prepare the proclamation for his signature. At left is Mrs. Henry Waldo Coe, a coworker in the feminist movement. (BELOW) In the early years of her campaign, Mrs. Duniway often traveled by stage coach. Such trips were usually uncomfortable and tedious, not nearly as exciting as this promotion picture from a handbill of the California & Oregon Stage Company. (*Both Oregon Historical Society*)

(ABOVE) A frequent scene during the steamboat era. The fast stern-wheeler *Bailey Gatzert* navigates a stretch of rough water in the swift-flowing Columbia River. (BELOW) The sidewheeler *Lot Whitcomb*, first steamer built on the Willamette River. She was launched in 1850 and was the first Northwest boat captained by Captain John C. Ainsworth. (*Both Oregon Historical Society*)

Captain John C. Ainsworth, who progressed from master to head of a
giant steamboat monopoly on the Columbia River, as he appeared in
his later years. (*Oregon Historical Society*)

(ABOVE) A crew of ranch hands employed by Pete French, Southeast Oregon cattle king, have lunch by their chuck wagon. Evidently this was a special occasion, as there are women visitors and the men are better dressed than when working. (BELOW) This is the big house, called the "White House," which Pete French built on "P" Ranch for his wife, who shunned it. The trees were planted to protect the house from the strong winds which blow across the semi-arid country. (*Both Oregon Historical Society*)

Pete French was a small man but energetic and imaginative. He was
shot fatally in an altercation with a homesteader. (*Oregon Historical
Society*)

(ABOVE, LEFT) This is the burro or jackass that is credited in folklore with discovering the Bunker Hill and Sullivan mine in Idaho. Harry Baer, partner of "Dutch Jake" Goetz, presented the picture to the mining company and said it was the only authentic one of the animal. (*The Bunker Hill Company*) (ABOVE, RIGHT) Noah Kellogg was a destitute old prospector when he and his burro uncovered the rich lode of galena which still is being worked in northern Idaho. This photo was made in his later life at Kellogg, Idaho, the town named for him. (*Kellogg Evening News*) (BELOW) Early day miners pose for photograph before going to work underground at Bunker Hill and Sullivan mine. (*The Bunker Hill Company*)

(ABOVE) General O. O. Howard, one-armed Civil War veteran, shown here in dress uniform in photo made at Vancouver, W.T., matched wits and military skill with Chief Joseph of the Nez Perces. The Army finally won, but General Howard had to admit the untrained Indian chief was as fine a general as he ever fought. (RIGHT) Chief Joseph was a peace-loving In-dian leader, but he finally was driven to war in an effort to save his beloved Wallowa Valley for his people. (*Both Oregon Historical Society*)

Jim O'Sullivan, who led the campaign for construction of Grand Coulee Dam in Washington, posed for this photograph by the spillway of the dam soon after it was completed. (*Portland Oregonian*)

(Mark Twain) how to pilot a side-wheeler through uncharted currents of the Mississippi River. Now he was to be the *Whitcomb*'s master. He understood better than most that her one-hundred-forty horsepower engine and her design were admirably suited to the Willamette and Columbia rivers.

To the taciturn, handsome young captain, whose side whiskers waggled in the wind as he surveyed her, it seemed remarkable that Lot Whitcomb could have produced so fine a vessel. Ainsworth didn't have a high regard for the man who had hired him a few months earlier in Sacramento (where the lonely captain had gone after the death of his first wife Josephine). Whitcomb was enterprising and ambitious, which was all right, for so was Ainsworth. But he was also "very vain, with very little education, and not entirely reliable." He had let Ainsworth know that he didn't need the latter's help or advice during the construction period.

The quiet young captain must have stood to one side, with a sardonic smile on his face, as the proprietor of Milwaukie gloried in the praise heaped upon him. The territorial legislature had officially chartered the boat as the *Lot Whitcomb of Oregon,* and Governor Gaines made the official christening speech at three o'clock. Mayor Kilbourne of Milwaukie also spoke and presented Mr. Whitcomb with a set of colors, donated by the people of Oregon City. The army band played "The Star-Spangled Banner" and "Hail Columbia." Mr. Whitcomb responded in his "usual and happy style," according to his own paper, the Milwaukie *Western Star.*

Then, as the *Lot Whitcomb* slid gracefully into the water, cannons were fired. Unfortunately one of these, on the schooner *Merchantman,* had become rusty from lack of care and exposure to the elements. When Captain Morse touched it off, it exploded. A jagged piece of cast iron struck the captain on the neck and nearly decapitated him. He died instantly.

This put a damper on the festivities, but did not quench them. The grand ball was held that night as scheduled. The dress uniforms of the officers from Vancouver made a colorful background for the gowns of Oregon Territory's society. Their brass buttons were a splendid complement to the brass band. The celebration lasted three days.

The *Lot Whitcomb* was, as we have seen, the first steamboat built on the Willamette River, but she was *not* the first built in Oregon. In the spring of 1850, James Frost and General John Adair constructed the ninety-foot *Columbia* at Astoria. She was, in Captain Ainsworth's eyes, a "small apology for a steamboat." He took passage on her from Astoria to Portland when he arrived in Oregon early in September, paying twenty dollars fare, and spent two nights aboard. The only part of her he considered safe for sleeping was next to the paddle box on the upper deck. The boat listed "several streaks" every time a passenger walked from one side to the other, and a sleeping person might easily slide off into the river.

Nevertheless the slow (four or five knots) *Columbia* was a big improvement over the sailboats, bateaux and canoes that had served the settlements before her time. She received a loud welcome when she arrived in Portland the Fourth of July on her maiden voyage. Later that evening an equally noisy greeting was repeated at Oregon City.

Captain Ainsworth soon, however, proved the *Lot Whitcomb* much the better vessel. He took her from Astoria to Oregon City in the remarkably short time of ten hours. He ran from Milwaukie to Oregon City in less than an hour. But the *Columbia* cut her rates and remained as a competitor. For a while there wasn't much business for the *Whitcomb*. If it hadn't been for towing lumber vessels up and down the Columbia, she wouldn't have even paid expenses.

Excursions run to islands and seldom-visited channels in the wilderness also helped buy the many cords of wood she consumed. The moon was as alluring then as it is today; young people responded with enthusiasm to the opportunities the *Whitcomb* offered for romantic night cruises.

Not long after the *Lot Whitcomb* went into service she ran aground on a reef at the mouth of the Clackamas River. Some historians have implied that the able, young Ainsworth was at the wheel when it happened. His memoirs deny this.

It seems that Mr. Whitcomb had asked Ainsworth to take a lesser job than master, such as supercargo or purser, so that a man named Hanscombe, the builder of the vessel, could have the captaincy. Ainsworth refused. But one week end, while Ainsworth was at the farm of Judge S. S. White, his future father-in-law, Whitcomb and Hanscombe decided to do what the captain said was impossible. Ainsworth had told them the river was too low to take so large a boat to Oregon City. Well, they would show the young skippersnapper it could be done!

Monday morning, as Ainsworth was riding into town on horseback from the White farm, he heard a loud puffing in the Willamette near the mouth of the Clackamas. Detouring to the river bank he saw the *Lot Whitcomb* stuck on a gravel bar. He knew that the river was dropping and that the vessel would remain aground for a long time. So he rode back to the farm to await developments.

It was not long, he recalled, before Mr. Whitcomb sent for him, asking that he take over and refloat the boat.

"I won't take over again until the boat is back where I left her!" the independent young skipper declared.

And so the *Lot Whitcomb* sat on the bar for a week or two until the river rose and floated her off. Mr. Whitcomb was understandably angry with Ainsworth. He kept Hanscombe on as master for several months, while Captain Ainsworth cooled his heels and courted Judge White's comely daughter Jane.

The *Lot Whitcomb* did make it to Oregon City not long after her first misadventure on the Clackamas reef. A poem written by Elizabeth Markham, mother of the famous Edwin Markham, shows how the coming of the steamboats filled Oregonians with elation. Published in the *Oregon Spectator* at Oregon City, Mrs. Markham's paean read:

> Lot Whitcomb is coming!
> Her banners are flying—
> She walks up the rapids with speed;
> She ploughs through the water,
> Her steps never falter—
> Oh! that's independence indeed.
> Old and young rush to meet her,
> Male and female to greet her,
> And waves lash the shore as they pass.
>
> Oh! she's welcome, thrice welcome
> To Oregon City:
> Lot Whitcomb is with us at last.
> Success to the Steamer,
> Her Captain and crew.
> She has our best wishes attained.
> Oh! that she may never
> While running this river
> Fall back on the sand bar again.

But presently Whitcomb and the other owners, among them Colonel Berryman Jennings of Sacramento, struck financial shoals. They had to sell the boat to an Oregon City firm. Captain Ainsworth, who had $3500 coming to him from the owners, received an interest in her for that amount and was made captain once again.

John Ainsworth (or J.C., as he was best known) could read a riffle better than most navigators today can read a chart. This he was to prove in many parts of the Northwest. But even he ran into trouble at times. One of those times was New Year's Day, 1853.

Heavy winter rains frequently push the Willamette out of its banks. On this occasion the river was rising rapidly—about a foot an hour. The current was like a millrace.

Captain Ainsworth attempted to take the *Lot Whitcomb* from Oregon City down to Milwaukie and soon regretted it. The boat was unmanageable in the racing current. Just above Milwaukie she was thrown broadside into Elk Rock. Water poured into her hull. Ainsworth and Jacob Kamm, the engineer, barely had time to run her to the left bank and get a line on a tree before she sank.

For a month, the master and his crew worked feverishly to salvage the *Whitcomb*. After the river had dropped some, they managed to get a patch on her and pump her out. A foot of sand had been deposited in the hold and on the main deck, and great trees hurtling down the river had broken and carried away much of the upper works. But by February 3 the *Whitcomb* was running again.

The young skipper was a serious man and he was very good with figures. Orphaned at eleven, he had lived with relatives in Ohio and Iowa. At thirteen he became bookkeeper as well as boy-of-all-work in an uncle's store. Later he became a successful merchant himself.

Undoubtedly, the captain did a lot of figuring as he stood hour after hour at the wheel of the *Lot Whitcomb*. The Oregon Steam Navigation Company, which was to make him and several others millionaires, probably was born in his imaginative mind during these hours.

However, "Jack" was not entirely a dull "boy." He liked to play a little, too. Play on any river during the steamboat era was likely to take the form of a race. Rival captains tried to outmaneuver each other, and their engineers risked boiler explosions by shutting the safety valves so that all the steam would go to the engines and the paddle wheels. Ainsworth never blew up a boat, but he did have some exciting races.

One was with the iron-hulled propeller boat *Willamette*, which had entered the Astoria–Oregon City service as a rival to the *Whitcomb*. The *Willamette* was a fast vessel and served admirably as a connecting boat with the steamships from San Francisco which put in at Astoria.

One day Captain Ainsworth brought his boat to the landing in Portland just as the *Willamette* was preparing to depart downriver. The propeller boat started off "like a streak" just before the *Whitcomb* had completed her loading of passengers and freight. Ainsworth took out after her, his side wheels threshing the water into foam. At the mouth of the Willamette River, the side-wheeler had almost caught the propeller boat. As the vessels entered the Columbia, Ainsworth pulled ahead by cutting close to shore, risking grounding or impalement on a submerged snag. Passengers on both boats cheered, and the race continued bow-and-stern all the way to St. Helens, where the *Willamette* had to stop to send a passenger ashore in a small boat.

Meanwhile, many steamers had been built or brought to the river. The *Lot Whitcomb* was more expensive to operate than some of the newer, smaller boats, and her owners decided to sell her in California. Ainsworth rode her down the coast in tow of the steamship *Patonia*. It was a rough voyage and by the time they arrived in San Francisco Bay the *Whitcomb* was leaking badly. He made temporary repairs and sold her for $40,000. With his share of the proceeds and with savings, he now had $4000—enough, he figured, to go into partnership with Jacob Kamm and Thomas Pope in the building of another boat.

This was the first stern-wheeler in Oregon. She was named the *Jennie Clark*, and Ainsworth had a quarter interest in her. He ran the *Jennie* between Portland and Oregon City, and he ran her hard.

"I was after success and was *bound to secure it*, if application and hard work would do it," the captain wrote in his memoirs many years later.

He frequently used Indians as deckhands, and when pressed for time at a landing, he would come down from the pilot house and lead his crew in carrying sacks of produce on his shoulders.

It was in this period that the future ruler of a steamboat empire first got rid of a competitor by buying him out. Many boats were on the rivers, but one, the *Relief*, made the skipper of the *Jennie Clark* especially hot under his high, stiff collar. The captain of the *Relief* was, in Ainsworth's words, "a blustery fellow, more intent on currying favor with the public than in making money for his owners." Ainsworth finally persuaded the principal owner of the *Relief* to sell his interest to him and his partners. Then he sent for the blustery master of the *Relief*, who hadn't heard about the transaction.

Ainsworth had a long talk with his "competitor," trying to convince him that the boats should make some arrangement for a division of business and profits. But the *Relief*'s master wouldn't hear of it. Finally the latter pulled his big, gold watch from his pocket and looked at it. "Sorry," he said. "It's time for me to shove off for Portland. I've got to get going."

"Don't rush off," Ainsworth told him. "You don't have to go to Portland. I've got a shorter trip than that for you."

"Shorter trip? What do you mean, *you've* got a shorter trip for me?"

"I mean that I've bought your boat and I want you to take her down to the lower end of town and lay her up," said Ainsworth icily.

The captain of the *Relief* lost his bluster. He yielded gracefully, Ainsworth recalled, making only a few remarks about this harsh treatment.

During the steamboat era, the Columbia River like Gaul, was divided into three parts—the upper, middle and lower. Celilo Falls was the dividing line between the upper and middle parts. Swift rapids called the Cascades separated the middle and lower stretches. Later canals and locks were built to permit steamers to pass from one section of the river to another, and, in recent years, power dams, equipped with navigation locks, have made the Columbia a series of slack-water pools.

But in the heyday of the steamboat it was customary to travel up or down the river in three stages. Going upstream from Portland, one boat would carry passengers and freight to the Cascades. There the people and cargo would be portaged around the rapids first by wagon and later on a wooden-rail tramway. The "Pony," the Northwest's first steam locomotive, ran on this primitive track. At this point there was a portage on each side of the river.

Above the Cascades, another steamboat took aboard passengers and freight, carrying them some forty miles to The Dalles. There another portage was necessary. A third boat waited above Celilo to carry travelers and cargo to destinations farther upstream.

The Indian war of 1855–56 created the first big demand for steamer transportation on the Columbia above Portland. The boats carried soldiers and military supplies in great number, including Lieutenant Phil Sheridan's dragoons from Fort Vancouver, by then a U.S. Army post. The Portages at the Cascades were the scene of one of the bloodiest episodes in the war. Sixteen white people were killed or died of wounds and twelve others were wounded.

Ainsworth had run the *Jennie Clark* about three years when he decided to sell his interest in her and build another steamer, the *Carrie Ladd*. While she was being built, he had an opportunity to poke about in strange waters.

R. R. Thompson, an upriver boatman, built a small craft, called the *Venture*, at the upper Cascades. After the boat was launched, Thompson invited a number of friends and hired a brass band for the maiden voyage to The Dalles. Thompson's partner, L. W. Coe, was in command. Captain Coe knew a lot about sailing bateaux on the upper river, but he didn't have much experience with steamboats. Before the engineer had got up enough steam to buck the current, the tyro skipper ordered the lines cast off. Instead of proceeding upriver toward The Dalles, the *Venture* drifted downstream into the rapids and struck a rock, brass band and all. The boat filled with water. One frightened guest leaped overboard and drowned. The rest were taken off in small boats.

After a while the river rose and the *Venture* floated off the rock. She was hauled ashore and repaired, and her name was changed to the *Umatilla*. Having no use for her on the lower river and being unable to take her over the Cascades, Thompson sold two-thirds of her to Ainsworth and a firm named Leonard and Green. There was a gold rush on the Fraser River in British Columbia, and the new owners saw an opportunity to make a tidy profit in those waters.

In July, 1858, the *Umatilla* left Astoria for Victoria, with

Ainsworth in command, in tow of the steamship *Columbia*. Ainsworth had steam on his boat to help move the two vessels over the rough bar. But outside in the ocean, where she was never designed to run, it was equally rough in the teeth of a fierce norther. The steam pipes on the *Umatilla* were twisting dangerously, and Ainsworth ordered his fires extinguished. His big supply of wood fuel was thrown overboard, and the paddle wheel was disconnected. Though she was lightened and the danger of fire and explosion averted, the little river boat still appeared doomed. The "hog chains" (cables stretched over posts above deck to resist vertical strains) parted and were replaced with heavy manila rope. Stairways twisted apart. That night at the wheel was "the longest" Ainsworth ever experienced. But daybreak found the boat still afloat and the sea quieter. Eventually the vessel arrived at Victoria, "but in a very dilapidated condition, oakum hanging out of every seam and the upper works very much injured."

After ten days, the *Umatilla* was repaired sufficiently for her first voyage to the Fraser. Crossing the Strait of Georgia, Captain Ainsworth picked up an Indian pilot who couldn't understand English. By following the Indian's signs and reading the new currents from old experience, the American made the run to Fort Langley at night. Later he reached Fort Hope, the farthest point a steamer had gone up to that time. But Fort Yale, twelve miles farther up the Fraser, was where most of the miners on board wished to go. So Ainsworth undertook to do what no steamboatman had ever done before.

It was touch-and-go. At Emory's Bar the *Umatilla* needed fifty-eight minutes to run a rapids one hundred yards long. The Fraser was lined with miners. When the little boat managed to edge forward a few feet, the men on the banks fired pistols and cheered. Then the boat would drop back a little and the noise on shore abated. Having "bottled up a little more steam," the boat would inch ahead again, and the shooting and shouting were renewed. The captain and crew received a warm welcome, indeed, when they finally landed at Fort Yale.

Even more thrilling to Captain Ainsworth was a subsequent voyage to the mining region by way of Harrison Lake, a shorter route but one which no steamer had attempted up to that time. The *Umatilla* reached the mouth of the Harrison River late in the afternoon. Many years later, aging and ill, Ainsworth jotted down his experiences for his children to read. He recalled his excitement at entering this unknown river. He wrote:

The sensation to me, of entering a water that had never before been divided by the prow of a steamer, was beyond description. The excitement and pleasure was always very great. In this particular instance it was doubly so, because we could get no reliable information about the river and were told by many that the Indians were very hostile to all white men.

Proceeding under slow-bell and with the lead line in constant use, the *Umatilla* felt her way up the river into a beautiful little lake. At the far end, the captain made out an Indian village. Were these the hostile redmen he had heard about? Would they ambush the steamer when she passed into the narrow stream connecting this body of water with the much larger Harrison Lake? Ainsworth thought not, for he could see women and children—and many dogs—about the village. If the Indians meant to attack him, they would have sent the women and children to a safe hiding place.

So he steamed boldly up the lake. He could see that the women and children were extremely agitated by the strange sight of a steamboat. Someone suggested he blow the whistle as the boat approached the village. Ainsworth pulled the cord. At the sound children and dogs stampeded wildly.

The big lake presented a grand sight when the *Umatilla* got there at dark. Ainsworth guessed it was forty miles long and in places five miles wide. The lake was completely surrounded by mountains that appeared to be thousands of feet high. On some of them snow could be seen. A full moon came up, apparently out of the water, and passengers and crew shouted with pleasure at the gorgeous sight.

Captain Ainsworth managed to appear concerned only with the safe operation of his vessel, but he found that it was difficult not to let himself go as his companions had.

"I am not as a rule very demonstrative myself, but I confess to have felt an enthusiasm on this occasion that was entirely new," he admitted in his memoirs.

Back on the Columbia, in the pilot house of his new *Carrie Ladd*, the poker-faced steamboatman found competition keen. There were too many boats for the amount of cargo and number of passengers. In familiar waters now, Ainsworth had time to use the calculating ability he had developed as a boy bookkeeper. If owners of boats on the three sections of the river could get together in a joint operation, he figured, they could provide service so good that they could capture nearly all the business.

He worked out an organization called the Union Transportation Line. On the lower river were his own *Carrie Ladd* and the *Mountain Buck*. On the middle river, the *Hassaloe* made connections for The Dalles. On the upper river, Thompson and Coe had just built the first steamboat above Celilo, the *Colonel Wright*. But the Union Transportation Line did not prove to be as airtight an organization as Ainsworth had hoped. The portage owners were not in it, and they controlled the traffic.

In 1860, therefore, the Oregon Steam Navigation Company was incorporated. This time the organizers, headed by Ainsworth, controlled not only a dozen steamboats, but the portages as well. When competition appeared, the O.S.N. cut its rates. After a few weeks or months, the competitors were forced to pull out; they couldn't meet the low rates and remain in business. Then the O.S.N. increased its charges to the earlier level, which was high: $8 per passenger and $20 per ton of freight from Portland to The Dalles, $18 per passenger and $90 per ton from Portland to Wallula (old Fort Walla Walla).

The O.S.N. had been in business only a few months when gold was discovered in Idaho. Instead of the expected few hundred passengers and a few tons of freight, the steamers carried 10,500 persons and 6290 tons of freight in the company's first full year of operation. At the height of the gold rush in 1864, they moved 36,000 passengers and 21,834 tons of freight between Portland and The Dalles. Profits that year totaled $783,339, a fabulous return on an original investment of $172,500. More and larger boats were required to handle the traffic, and some of the new vessels were veritable floating palaces.

Captain Ainsworth and his partners were not alone in profiting by the rush eastward from Portland. The interior, which an early-day clergyman and educator, George Henry Atkinson, had aptly labeled the "Inland Empire," gradually was settled by wheat growers and cattlemen. Soon wheat by the hundreds of thousands of bushels began pouring down the Columbia, from Idaho and eastern Washington and eastern Oregon, to make Portland one of the world's great grain ports. The city's harbor at the end of the harvest season was a forest of masts, as sailing vessels from all parts of the world gathered there to load wheat brought down the Columbia by steamers and later by rail.

Steamers pushed far inland to carry the gold miners to the mining camps. Captain Leonard White, who had piloted a steamboat as far as Eugene on the Willamette, steamed up the Snake River, past present-day Lewiston, Idaho, and up the Clearwater almost to its forks. He was master of the *Colonel Wright,* the Thompson and Coe boat which had become a part of the O.S.N. fleet. Ainsworth, incidentally, was one of the first men to visit Lewiston. He helped name it, for Meriwether Lewis of the Lewis and Clark expedition. Clarkston, Washington, across the river, was named for the other member of the exploring team.

A story was told, involving Len White, which demonstrated Captain Ainsworth's business acumen. Ainsworth was known all along the river as an employer who paid his employes well and treated them fairly. But Thompson and Coe had paid White $500 a month, a whopping big wage in those days. It was much too high, in Ainsworth's view, and he told White his pay would be cut to $300, the same as other O.S.N. skippers received. White quit. He went north to the Canadian border, where a new gold strike had been reported, and built himself a boat. Surprisingly, his financial backer was Captain Ainsworth.

Not all the O.S.N. endeavors were as profitable as its original one. The *Shoshone,* built at Fort Boise on the upper Snake, above Hells Canyon, did little business and was tied up on the river bank for three years. Then, under orders from Ainsworth, Captain Sebastian Miller and Chief Engineer Dan Buchanan took her through the roaring rapids of the deepest canyon in the whole United States. She got through to Lewiston, wracked and patched, and was sent on down the Columbia, over the falls at Celilo and through the Cascades, with

Captain Ainsworth himself at the wheel. She was sold and taken around the falls of the Willamette at Oregon City on skids. Then in the comparatively quiet Willamette she struck a rock and sank. A farmer made a chicken house out of her cabin.

The company's attempt to serve mining camps in Montana, by way of the Columbia and Snake rivers, a portage to Lake Pend Oreille in Idaho and another portage to the Clark Fork, was unsuccessful. The mining boom collapsed, and the company was left with three idle boats on the lake and on Clark Fork.

Then there was the *Oneonta*, the company's first palatial boat on the middle river. She proved too expensive to operate. In 1870, Captain Ainsworth, his side whiskers turning a little gray by now, ran her through the Cascades himself so that she could be used on the more densely populated lower river. He proved he was still a first-class steamboatman. He missed all the rocks, including the one on which Captain Coe had run the brass band aground.

Steamboats operated for nearly a century on the waters of the Northwest. But their heyday ended with the coming of the railroads.

On the Willamette, the first train chugged south from Portland to Oregon City on Christmas Day, 1869, passing by the launching site of the *Lot Whitcomb* just nineteen years to the day after Captain Ainsworth's first northwest command glided into the water. This railroad marked a severe defeat for Ainsworth, as well as for many others. For they too had sought to build a railroad, with government land grants, on the west side of the Willamette. Ben Holladay, a true buccaneer, had beat them to a frazzle by building on the east side and by winning the grants.

On the Columbia, a decade was to pass before a railroad spelled gradual doom to the steamboats. Henry Villard, German-born railroad builder and financier, saw that a line along the Columbia would be a link in a transcontinental setup, either with the Northern Pacific or the Union Pacific. In 1879, for five million dollars he bought out the O.S.N., including its portage railways, boats and wharves. The investment of $172,500 had paid off handsomely in less than twenty years, due largely to Captain Ainsworth's sharp figuring in the pilot house.

The Oregon Railroad & Navigation Company, the new name of the concern, operated steamboats until 1916, some of them splendid examples of the boat builder's art, but the emphasis was more and more on railroading. Many elderly folk still remember the steamboats of the O.R. & N., now a part of the Union Pacific. A few still living may recall as children the swift white boats of the Oregon Steam Navigation Company. Some of them may even have ridden on a boat steered by Captain J. C. Ainsworth himself.

Railroads did not kill off river traffic entirely. Gradually steamers were replaced by diesel tugs and barges. In the process the woodyard, a colorful appendage of steamboating, disappeared.

Early steamers used cordwood for fuel because it was plentiful and cheap. Every few miles, along the banks of the rivers, were cordwood piles, tended by tobacco-chewing men in wide-brimmed hats and their mournful-looking hound dogs. The woodmen were called "Pikes," perhaps because many of them came from Pike County, Missouri.

Wood burns rapidly, so a steamboat had to stop often for fuel. As she would nose into the bank the men on shore and the deckhands on board would transfer with remarkable speed several cords from land to the freight deck of the boat. Each boat or line had its own fuel supplies. Sometimes in a spirit of fierce competition, one boat's "Pikes" would destroy or steal another's woodpile. Bloody battles occasionally were fought over the great stacks of cordwood.

Usually a few pitchy knots were taken aboard with a pile of wood. These the engineer would set aside in the engine room. When a boat approached a landing, the captain blew the whistle several times. After a crowd had assembled at the landing, the engineer tossed a few pitchy pieces on the fire to make a black smoke. Captain Ainsworth had a reputation for excelling at that kind of showmanship.

Just as the steamboats were more glamorous than today's diesel tugs and barges, so the fragrant woodpile on the beach was more alluring than the odorous gas dock of the present.

John C. Ainsworth moved to California in 1880, hopeful that the warmer, drier climate would improve his health. For many years "J.C." had suffered from "dyspepsia." Today his ailment probably would be diagnosed as ulcers, and doctors would suggest that emotional stresses were responsible. Evidently, the calculating, taciturn captain paid dearly for being "after success" and being "bound to secure it."

He built a fine home near Oakland for his third wife, Fanny, daughter of General Edwin Babbitt, U.S.A. His second wife, Jane, had died in 1863. Captain Ainsworth had one son by his second marriage and six children by his third. Between severe illnesses he continued active in business both in California and in the Northwest. He died at his California home on December 30, 1893, forty-three years and five days after the launching of the *Lot Whitcomb*.

8 · PETE FRENCH—
CATTLE KING

An exhausted, half-frozen cowboy slid stiffly off a sweat-stained horse by the Southern Pacific depot at Winnemucca, Nevada, on the third day after Christmas, 1897. His heavy clothing was covered with snow and alkali dust, but he didn't stop to brush them off. He stumbled into the waiting room as fast as his numb legs could carry him.

"Pete French is dead!" he exclaimed to the telegraph operator behind the wicket. "A man shot him in the head! You've got to send word to his folks in Red Bluff!"

This was startling news. In this part of the West, the biggest cattle king was Pete French, a dapper, dark, little man who in a quarter-century had parlayed a thousand head of cattle into two million dollars on the lush grasslands of southeast Oregon.

Before he pounded out the news on his wire, the Morse operator made certain it was true. To him and to others in authority, the cowpoke told his story.

The young man was Dave Crow, a vaquero on Pete French's big spread in the valley of the Donner und Blitzen River. On Sunday, the day after Christmas, he related, French and his crew had gathered at the Big Sagebrush field at Sod House on Malheur Lake. Next day they were to start the long winter drive of three thousand fat steers to Winnemucca, two hundred fifty miles away.

French had just opened the gate to the field and turned his horse around to ride back and help his vaqueros start the cattle moving. A strange horseman appeared suddenly, seemingly out of nowhere, and the men, from a distance, noticed that he and French were arguing.

"Mr. French seemed to be trying to drive the man away—back the way he came," said Crow.

But the stranger didn't leave, so after a time French turned and started to ride off himself. The man followed at a distance of fifteen or twenty steps. Then he raised an arm, a shot rang out and French fell from his horse. The ranch owner was dead, a bullet in his head, when his men reached him. The stranger disappeared, and so far as young Crow was aware, no one knew who he was.

Crow remained at the scene only five minutes. Then he started south to make the long ride alone to Winnemucca and to tell the world about the crime. He followed the rough trail through sagebrush and dry lake beds that the cattle drive would have taken. He had been in the saddle forty-eight hours without sleep, stopping only to borrow fresh mounts, to gulp strong coffee and tell ranchers in lonely valleys of French's slaying. He had stopped nine times between Sod House and the railroad.

Dave Crow was bundled off now to Pete French's own quarters at the Winnemucca Hotel. While he slept, the news went out over the wires, not only to Red Bluff but to all parts of the West as well.

This was a front-page story. In Portland, *The Oregonian* followed the brief dispatch from Winnemucca with a lengthy review of Pete French's career. The editors were not overly surprised that French had been killed. He had engaged in frequent and bitter disputes with settlers over land claims, the paper recalled, and several times had been the "target of some of his opponents' rifle balls."

At the time no one realized that an era, as well as a cattle king, had come to a violent end. Though cattle by the hundreds of thousands continued to be produced in southeast Oregon, never again would a single man dominate that region.

Pete French arrived in Oregon in 1872. He was only twenty-three years old then, but already he had demonstrated an audacity and self-assurance that more than made up for his tiny five-foot-five, one-hundred-thirty-pound frame. For several years, after leaving his parents' small ranch near Red Bluff, he had worked at Jacinto, an old, sprawling Spanish land grant near Chico, California. Dr. Hugh J. Glenn ruled Jacinto like a Spanish grandee, and had quickly recognized a kindred spirit in the small, black-haired, black-eyed cowboy who had come to work for him.

Civilization was beginning to crowd the big landowners of California. Fence laws had been enacted; they restricted the running of huge herds of cattle on the open ranges. So Dr. Glenn was switching to grain. Soon he was to be the largest wheat grower in the United States, employing a thousand men to sow and reap a million bushels a year.

There were, however, still opportunities for big-scale cattle raising. Southeast Oregon had wide ranges and well-watered valleys where grass grew as high as a horse's belly.

Henry ("Hen") Owen, known as the "Oregon swamp rat," had spread the word among wealthy Californians that un-limited quantities of swampland could be bought in Oregon from the state for $1.25 an acre. He had acquired many acres himself, paying only one-tenth of the purchase price in cash, the rest on credit. Now he was willing to dispose of his land at a fair profit.

A man took a chance, of course, on receiving title to the land when the state got around to determining whether it was, in fact, swampland. But Hen had a scheme that would con-vince a not-too-skeptical land board. He would put a boat on a wagon and drive around the country while sitting in it. Then he could swear that he had covered the whole area in a boat.

One big cattle and horse raiser from the Chico area, John Devine, had already moved to Oregon, establishing ranches on the east side of Steens Mountain in Harney Valley. Dr. Glenn decided he would try to do so, too, but not in person. He made a partner of the up-and-coming young Pete and sent him off with more than a thousand cattle, across the Sierra and the deserts to start a second Jacinto.

With half a dozen Mexican vaqueros, two ranch hands, twenty horses, a cook and supply wagons, cocky little Pete French set out boldly. For weeks he led his entourage hundreds of miles across rugged and thirsty terrain. A sombrero was perched jauntily on his oversize head. The silver-mounted bridle on his horse glinted in the sun.

On the west side of Steens Mountain where the Donner und Blitzen pours from the long-lasting snow of the mountain range, he found just what he wanted. The grass grew high in the valley and in the marshes, which deepen to form Harney and Malheur lakes. The unfenced range stretched to the horizon. Pete's black eyes must have gleamed as he pictured thousands of cattle grazing on these endless acres during the summer. In fall there would be plenty of grass and hay in the valley meadows to fatten the steers for market and to keep young cows and calves over winter.

He would build a big white house here, much like the one at Jacinto, for the luxury-loving Ella, Dr. Glenn's daughter, who had promised to become his wife.

Piute Indians roamed the country, and some white men, besides John Devine, were already there. But few of them were disposed to quarrel with the dapper young French about land and water. The only complaints came from the thousands of water fowl that had laid primary claim to the lakes and marshes since the ice age. They rose from the coarse marsh grass in scolding clouds as Pete and his men began to dig drainage ditches and build dams so that the land would produce more grass to fatten French-Glenn cattle.

The coyotes yipped on the ridges, but they weren't really complaining. The cattle French brought would have calves and a calf makes a tasty dinner for a coyote. The deer and the antelope didn't say anything. They just ran.

Pete had been in the Blitzen Valley only a short time when he bought out his first settler. The man was a prospector who also owned a few cattle. These he branded with the letter "P," because his name was Porter. He was disgusted with the isolated country and was glad to sell any claim he might have to the valley by right of prior occupancy. Along with his rights went his branding iron. Thus, Pete's headquarters place became the P Ranch, not from his first name, as one might guess, but because he had bought a secondhand iron shaped like a "P."

South of P Ranch, about sixteen miles, a settler named Ruby was running cattle and horses, using a diamond brand. French bought him out, too, paying between twenty and thirty thousand dollars, besides the price of the livestock. No title went with the deal, only Ruby's claim to possession by right of occupancy.

With his marshland, for which he had no title, either, and the open range, valuable only to the person who had access to water, French was well on the way to achieving his cattle kingdom. Eventually he controlled two hundred thousand acres, of which one hundred thousand were fenced with five hundred miles of wire. By 1878 he had twenty thousand head of cattle and a large number of horses, a fine spread for a man not yet thirty.

Pete was the region's best fence builder. This semiarid

country contains much rim rock, left over from an ancient geological age when streams cut into bedrock and left jagged walls of stone to rise above the soil of today's benchlands. Except for occasional breaks, rim rock makes a good natural fence, and French was quick to take advantage of this fact. He sent men to ride the ridges, looking for breaks. These they plugged with stones or juniper logs.

Before barbed wire came on the market, French built miles of plain wire fences. His men bored holes in juniper poles and strung wire through them. The poles were dug in as far as the rocky soil would permit. The youthful cattle king did more than stake out an empire; he fenced it!

French's corrals were admired as much as his fences. Juniper poles were set into the ground at close intervals and bound with rawhide. Then willow was woven into the framework much as one would make a wicker basket. The corrals stood for years, as strong as the day French and his buckaroos built them.

For his big White House (it was always referred to in capital letters) and his barns, French hauled lumber from the Blue Mountains, one hundred fifty miles away. Ten- and twelve-mule teams were constantly on the road pulling great wagons of boards when the master of P Ranch was building. They continued running long after that, bringing supplies to the French ranches and merchandise for a store Pete built to accommodate his hands at P Ranch. Winnemucca was the usual source of these supplies. It was a long haul over the desert, and from an elevation one could spot a freight wagon coming for many miles by the cloud of dust it raised.

As Pete French was doing west of Steens Mountain, so John Devine was doing on the east. He bought out settlers and other ranchers, got his hands to stake out homesteads and then sell the land to him, and by other means consolidated large holdings. French and Devine were friendly, however. Each was content to let the other have his own sphere of influence.

They were a strange pair. Devine was of "unusual" height and size. He towered over the five-foot-five French. He was a hearty, back-slapping man, whereas French was polite but aloof. When seen together, they must have reminded others of an amiable St. Bernard puppy and a rather short-tempered bantam rooster.

Though Devine was a horse fancier and spent much of his time and money developing race horses, which he raced on the dry bed of Alvord Lake, he usually traveled with buggy and team. Bill Hanley, who came to the country when French and Devine were in their prime, noted that Devine's buggy was built on the lines of an overland stagecoach, with rocker springs. It rode extremely high. The big, handsome Devine, sitting straight in this conveyance and holding the reins of a picked team of horses, never failed to arouse admiration.

To Hanley, French, on the other hand, looked like a dancing master. He was dapper, slim, wiry, quick to act and make decisions. He often carried a cane—like a swagger stick, one presumes. A black, bushy mustache offset any impression of femininity.

Even more of a contrast to French was "Colonel" Hardin, whose main ranch was on King River in Nevada but who was also part-owner of the OO Ranch near the French holdings. Hardin weighed three hundred and fifty pounds, possibly more, and stood six feet six. He had come riding up into the French-Devine country in a buckboard lengthened out to ten or twelve feet, with a high spring seat in the center. Here the giant sat, driving a huge team of horses with a chain harness whose jingling could be heard as far as one could see the rig. Hardin always had a jug of whisky on the seat beside him.

As a sixteen-year-old, striking out for himself, Hanley came upon a roundup in the Harney Basin. He was ragged and dirty after weeks of driving a small herd of cattle from west of the Cascades in southern Oregon. All the owners in the Harney Basin were present, including French and Devine. Hanley, who later became a big cattleman himself and even operated the P Ranch, got his first taste there of cattle-king hospitality. Though he represented possible competition for land and water, the cattlemen made him welcome.

The camp cook had just finished preparing supper as young Hanley rode up.

"Come and get it!" he yelled, and the vaqueros made a bee-line for the mess wagon.

Then one of the men noticed the ragged boy on his wornout mount. "Turn your horse loose, boy, and get yourself something to eat," he said. Hanley did, and camped with the big outfit overnight.

What struck the lad from western Oregon, as much as the hospitality, were the Spanish trappings, customs and terminology the Californians had brought to Oregon. Hanley was impressed too by the showiness of both bosses and vaqueros, many of the latter Mexicans. All were well dressed in bright colors. Every man was equipped with splendid, well-trained saddle horses whose bridles were silver-mounted. Over their clothes they wore *rosideros*, buckskin aprons fitting like tailored trousers and tied around the legs with buckskin thongs. Their hair ropes were called *mecates* and their long rawhide ropes for catching and throwing steers and calves were known as *riatas*.

Southeast Oregon became in fact an extension of old Mexican California. Cattlemen who arrived later from other parts of the country adopted the Californians' codes and methods. The Mexican vaquero was admired as much by the latecomer as by his own kind. The longer his *riata,* the greater his skill. Some of these rawhide ropes stretched seventy feet. The more fine saddle horses a rider had in his string, the higher was his rank. Some had as many as twenty mounts, in which they took great pride.

The Spanish tradition in the Northwest ended at the Blue Mountains in northeastern Oregon and at the Snake River. But, its influence was wider. The word "buckaroo," used universally where American cowboys ride, is traced to the Spanish. It is a corruption of "vaquero."

Some of the Mexicans brought up by the cattle kings from California became well-known characters in their own right. Such a one was Prim Tebo Ortego, Pete French's chief vaquero, who went to work for him in 1877. Tebo was still at P Ranch when French was shot.

Pete permitted Tebo to run a small herd of his own. The Mexican sold it at Winnemucca when French's cattle were marketed. Tebo, you see, had no ambition to become a cattle king. Money, in his view, was just something to spend. With cattle profits in his pocket, Ortego would take on the gamblers at Winnemucca. Invariably he lost but it took the gamblers a while to clean him. Then broke he would come back to P Ranch to start again from scratch. Admonished about this, Tebo shrugged his shoulders nonchalantly and exposed his white teeth in a grin.

"I make 'em work for it," he would say.

French expected his hired hands to earn their pay. But he himself labored as hard as any of them. Some riders started with Pete for as little as twenty dollars a month, others received fifty dollars. They respected the aloof, energetic, quick-tempered little man because he was fair to everyone. Not infrequently he rehired men who had quit after a foreman had made unreasonable demands. He kept men on after the winter drive, although there was little for them to do then. He rewarded loyalty, and nearly every man who worked for him was in fact loyal to him.

After the steers had been driven to market at Winnemucca in late fall or early winter, only cows with young calves and young heifers had to be fed hay at the ranch. Most winters the remaining cattle found adequate feed for themselves on the range. In late March or early April the busy season for French and his vaqueros began. Then the cattle which had wintered in the valley were driven out to the range.

Next came the roundup of horses and the branding of colts. When this was finished, it was time to round up the cattle and brand the unweaned calves. Crews from many ranches, whose cattle shared the same range, would work together, separating the cows bearing the various brands and the calves that stayed close by their mothers. It was such a roundup that young Hanley had chanced upon. The hands worked hard, but sometimes they had time too for impromptu bucking and roping contests. The camp cooks fed them well on venison as well as beef.

A spring roundup was something a stranger to the cattle country would never forget. Expertly, the cowboys cut out the steers from among the cows. Then they separated the unbranded calves from the cows, roping the calves and throwing them, but not too hard. The riders' horses were an intimate part of the team, both in cutting and roping; they moved quickly to head off a steer or held the rope at just the right tautness when a calf had been thrown.

Branding irons were kept hot in a bed of coals. After a calf had been caught, one man would slit its ear to mark it and another would press the hot iron to its left hip. The bawling of the animals drowned out the sizzle of the burning hide, but the pungent odor of burning hair and flesh could not be hidden. It filled the nostrils of both men and beasts.

Pete French not only drove his own cattle to market, but originated a marketing method that was practiced in southeast Oregon for a long time. In late November or December he would buy steers from other cattlemen and homesteaders, strictly on credit. These, with his own, he drove to Winnemucca and shipped by rail to San Francisco. There he sold the stock, and in January he returned with a satchelful of gold.

French traveled frequently to San Francisco, not only to sell cattle. He also went there to visit his wife Ella. The cultured Mrs. French did not come often to the White House he built for her at P Ranch, and when she came she did not remain long.

French had done everything he could to make the ranch attractive, but to no avail. Poplars grew in rows around the house to shield it from the strong winds that blew across the treeless plateau, for storms often were violent. The Donner und Blitzen River got its name from a thunder storm raging there as Colonel George B. Currey and his troops crossed it during the Snake Indian war of 1864.

The White House was always open to guests, and they were numerous. A big table was invariably set, and two cooks were ready to provide meals for any number of people. Cattlemen from three states often dropped in on Pete. Their various brands were burned into the wood around the huge fireplace as decoration.

Cattlemen, however, did not appeal to Mrs. French. She preferred the more cultured life of Jacinto or San Francisco. Finally she divorced Pete. Their son Glenn did not take to ranching, either. He was seldom in his father's company, and when he was old enough, he decided to become a scholar, rather than a rancher.

So Pete French was a lonely king in his castle. Vainly attempting to escape from loneliness he built his kingdom ever larger and larger. He became more and more aggressive toward the penniless settlers who arrived in their shabby covered wagons to file for homesteads on land he considered his own.

Before the violent conflict between cattlemen and homesteaders broke out, there had been war between whites and Indians. In this, all the white men, cattle barons and lowly homesteaders alike, had been on the same side. In this time of stress, Pete French, the diminutive master of the French-Glenn barony, became a hero by his decisiveness and courage.

Through much of the Northwest, in the middle and late 1870s, Indians were on the warpath. Sitting Bull and his Sioux warriors annihilated General George A. Custer and his troops on the Little Big Horn River in Montana. Peace-loving Chief Joseph of the Nez Perces finally rebelled against the white invaders who did not keep their promises. Then stirred by the early successes of Joseph, the Bannocks of southern Idaho also struck against the whites. They moved westward in the spring of 1878 into southeast Oregon and northern Nevada where the Piutes lived.

Some of the latter, under Chief Winnemucca of Nevada, refused to take part in the rebellion. But others, under handsome, six-foot Chief Egan, attacked the settlers around Steens Mountain, which the redmen hoped to regain for themselves.

Most of the settlers escaped to Camp Harney where a few soldiers remained of the troops under General O. O. Howard; they were chasing the Indians. Egan's men were more interested in stealing good saddle horses than in killing white men, but they burned ranch buildings besides collecting some two thousand horses.

Pete French and his vaqueros were at Diamond Ranch engaged in their spring roundup when Coon Smith, a settler, appeared riding fast from Happy Valley.

"The Indians are coming!" shouted Smith. Not far behind the settler French could see a scouting party tearing down Diamond Hill in hot pursuit. He yelled for his men, who were working in a corral, to grab their horses and head for P Ranch. Then Pete himself jumped to the top of the corral, grabbed Coon Smith's rifle and single box of cartridges and began shooting at the advancing Indians. This stopped the warriors long enough for the men to get away.

French knew the Indians would attack again, probably at a gap in the ridge through which the McCoy Creek Trail ran. Leaping on his own horse, he cut across country to the gap, arriving just in time to shoot at the advancing Indians from the cover of a rock. With this help, his men got through to P Ranch, except for the Chinese cook, who fell from his horse and was shot and scalped. Coon Smith's horse was cut from under him, but French saw the cook's horse running riderless and dragging a rope. He grabbed the rope and gave it to Smith with orders to mount. John Witzel, a young cowboy, was shot in the hip but managed to get through to P Ranch.

The men rode on to Camp Harney, arriving the next morning. Altogether they had ridden nearly one hundred miles. Now General Howard made French a courier and set out with his soldiers and civilian volunteers to track down the Indians. The white men found the OO Ranch burned and many of its horses stolen. The P Ranch, however, was still intact.

The pursuers caught up with Egan's warriors at Silver Creek and engaged in an indecisive pitched battle. Watching the fighting from behind General Howard's lines, Pete French caught sight of one of his favorite horses being ridden by an Indian. Apparently Pete lost his temper. He galloped up and down the line offering a reward to anyone who would shoot the offending Indian. No one did.

On this occasion Chief Egan escaped from Howard's men. But a short time later, some Umatilla Indians killed him and collected a reward. This was the last of the Indian wars. Sitting Bull, Joseph and Egan had all been defeated. Reluctantly the redmen retired to the reservations the white men had set up for them.

With the Indian wars over, the settlers came in greater numbers. Many filed for homesteads on land the cattle kings claimed as their own. French was able to buy out some of these newcomers and persuade them to leave the country. But Ed Oliver wouldn't give up his land, which lay in the middle of one of French's giant fields. French and Oliver had heated arguments about this on several occasions.

Some of French's disputes with the homesteaders resulted from receding water in Malheur Lake during a drought that lasted several years. The government had surveyed a line along the south shore of the lake some years earlier, and French had secured possession of the water front. As the lake receded, it became necessary to run a second line. Pete claimed everything up to the new line, but meanwhile others had taken possession of some of the land in between.

French filed many suits in court to dispossess the interlopers, but the decision was long in coming. Meanwhile, Commissioner Sparks of the General Land Office had permitted the settlers to remain on the land and some of them had made permanent improvements. When it was finally decided that the land was swampland and that it belonged to French, the dispossessed settlers were naturally indignant. Many meetings were held at Burns to find a way of saving the settlers' homes. Some settlers favored direct physical action against the cattle baron, whom they considered ruthless beyond reason.

French escaped harm, however, until the day after Christmas in 1897.

And even if Dave Crow didn't know who had shot his employer, the mystery was soon solved. Ed Oliver had fired the shot, and he admitted as much to Sheriff John McKinnon when the latter arrested him on December 27. Oliver surrendered the revolver with which he had felled the cattle king. One cartridge remained in the cylinder.

French's body lay on the ground where he fell until the next day, when Coroner T. W. Stephens arrived from Burns. Pete's sad vaqueros covered the corpse with two pieces of saddle blanket and a tent. William Gilliam, one of French's hands, stayed with the body all night, except when he went home for supper. After the coroner had examined the body, it was hauled away in a wagon. An inquest was held at Sod House Ranch that day, the twenty-seventh; the verdict was that French had died of a gunshot wound inflicted by Oliver.

Pete French rode out of his kingdom in a box lined with tin and padding, well sealed against freezing. A tarpaulin was thrown over the box to give it added protection. Mart Brenton and Bert French, the dead man's brother, drove the improvised hearse through snow to Baker City via Canyon City. On some of the steeper grades they had to hold the wagon back with poles. At Baker the body was embalmed. Then Wells Fargo Express took charge. Pete was shipped by rail to Portland, then south to Red Bluff, where he had been born not quite fifty years earlier.

Ed Oliver was indicted for manslaughter on May 18, 1898. Sheriff McKinnon served a bench warrant on him the same day. Eleven friends and neighbors furnished $10,000 bail.

In the dusty cowtown of Burns, trial began next day at the little courthouse. Between December and May, few residents of Harney County had remained indifferent. The homesteaders insisted Oliver must be freed; the cattlemen demanded his conviction. Sheepmen, however, tended to be neutral; they had fought with both factions.

The firm opinions of prospective jurors delayed the taking of testimony. Finally, on May 24, twelve men were sworn in as a jury. By that time, forty-five men had been examined.

The state called sixteen witnesses, the defense nineteen. Many of the witnesses for the state were vaqueros who had been at Sagebrush field with French on the fatal day after Christmas. They told much the same story that Dave Crow had related in the Winnemucca railroad station.

Then the defense introduced a large stick as evidence. It had been found in the field, and the defense implied that French had beaten Oliver with it before the shooting. French's vaqueros swore, however, that he had carried only a willow whip, the one he had cut that morning to drive two cows he and Arthur Cooper had pulled from the river.

French was unarmed, his cowboys swore. The body lay untouched, they asserted, until the coroner came. The coroner found no weapon on it.

The testimony of Prim Tebo Ortego, Pete's chief vaquero, was typical. As French rode around the cattle to open the gate between Sagebrush field and Wright field, Tebo testified, he saw Oliver coming from the north gate.

"French went out to him and motioned him back," said Tebo. "Oliver charged his horse on Mr. French. Mr. French turned his horse and Oliver charged again, as if trying to lunge past him. I saw Oliver go for his gun. Mr. French then turned and rode away. Oliver followed and raised his arm, then fired and Mr. French fell from his horse. I could not see the pistol, but I saw the smoke and heard the report. I was 191 yards from where Mr. French and Mr. Oliver had the difficulty. When I saw Oliver rush his horse, I stopped and watched."

The stick introduced by the defense was then shown to the witness.

"I could tell the difference between the whip and this stick!" declared Tebo. "He did not have this stick!

"Mr. French leaned forward and was looking back when the shot was fired. Oliver rode around to one side of French and looked down. Then he rode away."

Several defense witnesses now testified that they had heard French threaten Oliver on several occasions. "If I catch you in my field again, I'll fix you!" French told the homesteader, they insisted. The threat was embellished with curses. Several witnesses attempted to tell of altercations they themselves had had with French, but objections to that line of testimony were sustained by the judge. Then Mrs. Oliver was called to tell of the comings and goings of her husband on the day of the shooting. Defense attorneys brought out from her the fact that she had four small children.

The highlight of the trial, however, was Oliver's testimony in his own defense. He owned no lands in dispute with the French-Glenn Company, he said, but since the company's land completely surrounded his homestead, he had no road out. This situation had existed for three years. Altogether he had known French nine years, Oliver related, and had worked for him on and off for three years, the last time being three years before the shooting.

"We had a Christmas tree Christmas night," the homesteader said. "We were up late and I didn't get up until nine o'clock next morning. I left the house about eleven o'clock to get a horse from George Curtis' pasture. I stayed at Curtis' until after dinner, then started back to the Rock Ford place." (This was where Mrs. Simmons, his mother-in-law, lived and where the Olivers were staying.)

The homesteader went on to tell of threats made to him by French at a political convention in Burns two years before.

"Here, Oliver, is a bill for three hundred dollars," he quoted French as saying. "Pay that and you can have a road."

Then followed, according to Oliver, vicious curses and a declaration by French that "I'll shoot you first time I catch you going into that place."

Similar threats had been made on other occasions, said Oliver.

The homesteader then added that he didn't know French was around on the day of the shooting. He had heard that the cattleman had gone to Chicago with some stock before Christmas. The settlers had understood, he said, that they could come into French's field and get their cattle when French's crew was rounding up. Oliver heard cattle in the field, he testified, and rode to a slight elevation where he could see the animals. He entered Sagebrush field and rode south along the fence to learn if any cattle belonging to him or Mrs. Simmons were there.

"I was within two hundred yards of French when I first saw him," Oliver swore. "French stopped when he saw me, then he went out to the fence and got down. I thought he opened the gate. Then he came back around the cattle directly to me. I knew he carried a pistol. When he got within thirty or forty yards I saw he had a stick—I thought it was a whipstock.

"French said, 'You jug bellies harass me to death! I'll make an example of you!' He beat me and said, 'I'll kill you!' Then he reached for his gun. I jerked out my pistol and fired as quickly as possible. I did so because I thought he would kill me. . . . I only pulled the trigger once. . . ."

The jury retired at four o'clock to consider the evidence. Three hours later it returned to the tense court room. The clerk read the verdict, "Not guilty."

The verdict was greeted with "mixed emotions," wrote a Harney County historian. This was decidedly an understatement, for even today an account of Pete French's death is certain to bring forth conflicting versions from men who took either the settlers' side or that of the cattlemen.

A great part of Pete French's cattle kingdom has returned to its natural state now. In 1908, President Theodore Roosevelt set aside ninety-five thousand acres around Harney and Malheur lakes as the Malheur National Wildlife Refuge. In 1935, the federal government bought sixty-five thousand acres of the old P Ranch, including Pete's beloved White House, to add to the refuge, the largest of its kind in the world. A million birds a year, including ducks, geese, grebe, killdeer, avocets and innumerable other species, nest peaceably in the marshes where Pete French dug canals, built dams and argued with homesteaders. A small number of trumpeter swan, once almost extinct, are guarded zealously by the refuge staff.

Homesteading didn't prove profitable in the Steens Mountain area. But many cattle still graze on the range and in the valleys. A small store and hotel, called Frenchglen, preserve the names of the last of the cattle despots and his father-in-law. It's a fine country still, and prosperous, though thinly populated. Above all, peace reigns along the Donner und Blitzen. Today no one would attempt to rule there in the Pete French manner.

9 · ABIGAIL SCOTT DUNIWAY —
LIBERATOR OF WOMEN

When all the small children of the village had gathered in the shade of the big sycamore tree, the frail, little girl who had summoned them there climbed up on a limb. Then she made a campaign speech for William Henry Harrison.

The year was 1840 and the village was Wesley, Illinois, which lies on the east bank of the Illinois River south of Peoria. The little speech-maker was Abigail Jane Scott. She would be six years old in October. In November the men of the United States would go to the polls and elect General Harrison as their next President.

Abigail's father, John Tucker Scott, was a stanch Whig. This was also General Harrison's party. To the other children, the tyke in the long dress and sunbonnet repeated the arguments she had heard her father make. She shouted the catchy slogan, "Tippecanoe and Tyler Too," which helped the Whigs win the election that year. General Harrison had been the hero of a battle with the Indians at a place called Tippecanoe.

There is no record of Abigail's being punished for making the speech. Perhaps she was too small to be noticed. Not many years would pass, however, before she realized that members of the female sex who spoke in public were considered unwomanly. She would soon learn, too, that women couldn't vote and that in many other ways they were in the same category as "idiots, insane persons, criminals and Chinamen."

The first realization of the low estate of women came to Abigail as she watched her mother, Ann Roelofson Scott, decline in health. Twelve children were born to her parents;

nine of them survived infancy. The mother became a semi-invalid caring for her large family and working from sunup to long after dark at her innumerable household tasks.

Then on Abigail's tenth birthday, her mother told her how disappointed she had been when she was born, because Abigail was a girl. She was the second girl to come to the Scott household in seventeen months. And on a later occasion, when still another girl was born, the mother wept.

"Poor baby!" she sobbed. "She'll be a woman some day. Poor baby! A woman's lot is so hard!"

Abigail's father appears to have been a considerate husband by the standards of the time. But he made all the decisions for the family. His wife's opinions carried little weight.

Thus, in 1852, he caught the "Oregon fever," which had waxed and waned for more than a decade in the Illinois-Missouri region. Though his wife was in poor health, hardly able to care for the family in their comparatively comfortable home, he decreed that they should undertake the long, hard journey to Oregon. In April, the Scotts and their nine children set out by ox-drawn covered wagon.

Long, long afterward, the grief of her mother, as she visited for the last time the "hallowed spot in the pasture where the remains of her first-born son were buried," was indelibly engraved on Abigail's memory.

The frail, work-worn Mrs. Scott never saw Oregon. On June 20, she died on the plains of cholera, a disease of the trail to which she fell easy prey.

Abigail was seventeen years old at the time. Her brother Harvey, later famous as editor of the *Portland Oregonian*, was in his early teens. The tragedy made a strong impression on all the Scott children.

Years later, Harvey Scott told his sister that he still awakened sometimes at night thinking about their mother's hard life; he would rise and pace the floor of his bedroom.

"Yes, Brother," Abigail replied, "and her memory, added to my own experiences and those of our surviving sisters, led me long ago to dedicate these maturer years of my life to the enfranchisement of women."

Abigail learned herself about the hard lot of women soon after the family's arrival in Oregon. Although she had little formal schooling, the young woman had managed to educate herself sufficiently to obtain a job as teacher at Eola. She attributed much of her learning to a dog-eared copy of Webster's *Elementary Spelling Book;* she carried it with her across the plains. At Eola, then called Cincinnati, she met and married a young farmer named Benjamin C. Duniway. Two children were born within two and one-half years on the donation land-grant farm where Ben took his young bride.

Seventy years later Abigail tartly recalled her four years on this farm:

"It was a hospitable neighborhood composed chiefly of bachelors, who found comfort in mobilizing at meal times at the home of the few married men of the township," she wrote. Her husband was in his glory when entertaining these visitors at his fireside, Abigail recalled, while she, "if not washing, scrubbing, churning, or nursing the baby, was preparing their meals in our lean-to kitchen." To be a pioneer drudge, without a penny of her own, "was not pleasant business for an erstwhile schoolteacher, who had earned a salary. . . ."

Mr. Duniway sold the farm after four years and bought another in Yamhill County where the family lived five more years. There the young wife was as much of a drudge as ever. One day she was in the yard picking ducks for their feathers, with which to make pillows, when a man appeared and spoke to her husband at the woodpile where he was working. The man asked Ben to go surety on a loan for a considerable sum, with interest at 2 per cent a month, compounded semiannually. After talking for some time, the men entered the house.

Ben didn't consult his wife about the transaction. Under the law she was a nonentity. But she realized that the notes could spell financial ruin, and so she laid down the duck she was picking and went into the living room, her heart pounding.

"My dear, are you quite certain about what you are doing?" she asked her husband. He had already signed two notes and now signed a third.

"Mama, you needn't worry," he said. "You'll always be protected and provided for." Abigail bit her lips to keep silent and returned to her duck-picking.

The notes did prove their financial ruin. Crops failed; and a flood in the Yamhill River carried away a granary containing what little produce there was. The notes fell due. All the Duniways had left was a small piece of property in Lafayette. They had just moved to town when Ben was injured by a runaway team so severely that he could never again do hard physical labor. Abigail had to become the breadwinner now as well as the homemaker. She opened a private school and lined the unfinished attic with unbleached muslin as a dormitory for young lady boarders.

In summer she arose at three o'clock and in winter at four to do a day's housework before opening her school. Having had no opportunity to read the lessons beforehand, she kept one jump ahead of her pupils while they were reciting. At four o'clock each afternoon she was at her household duties again. Despite the hard work, she led an easier life than she had known on the farm.

After a time the Duniways moved to the larger town of Albany where Abigail again taught school until she thought she had enough money to open a millinery and notions store. But by the time she had converted her school into a store, she had just thirty dollars of capital left.

Fortunately, a Portland wholesaler, Jacob Mayer, gave her twelve hundred dollars worth of merchandise on credit. In three weeks Abigail paid the debt in full and received three thousand dollars worth of goods. She was never again to know poverty.

As a milliner, Abigail got a new look at woman's lowly estate.

The wife of one well-to-do farmer, who had just bought a valuable race horse, came to her shop to ask for sewing to do at home. The woman was in poor health, had one small baby and was expecting another. She had promised her older daughters waterproof suits to wear to Sunday school but *he* had taken her butter money to pay for the horse. The girls had complained so much about the suits that she felt she must find some way to buy them or go crazy. The woman died the next summer and the ministers of several churches offered the bereaved husband condolences from the pulpit.

"I, who had had a glimpse behind the scenes, pondered long and deeply over that 'butter money,' the defrauded children, the deceased wife and that thoroughbred race horse," recalled Abigail.

On a different occasion another woman came to the millinery store in tears. Her husband had sold their household furniture and disappeared, leaving her with five small children and no money. Abigail arranged with a friend to lend the woman money in order to rent a house where she could take in boarders. The little boardinghouse business was just well under way when the husband returned and took possession of everything, repudiating the mortgage which his wife had no legal right to contract. Her only recourse was the divorce court.

Then one bright spring day a husband, wife and four small daughters drove up to the store in a fine carriage. They were looking for hats for the girls and Abigail took down from the shelves some prettily trimmed "Neapolitans." She kept the husband in pleasant conversation while the wife selected four hats.

"What's the damage?" asked the man when the choice had been made.

"Four hats, at three dollars each, will be twelve dollars," the milliner replied.

"That's more money than I can spare for children's hats!" the father declared. "Haven't you anything cheaper?"

Abigail took down some hats of woven fiber which she kept in stock for berry pickers. These were "six bits" apiece.

"They'll do," the man said.

The girls protested, but their mother shook her head at them, then sweetly asked her husband to go to another store where she had forgotten to pick up a butter firkin.

After the husband had left, the woman told Abigail to wrap up the four Neapolitans. The amazed shopkeeper asked if the husband wouldn't know the difference.

"No! He doesn't know any more about a hat than I know about a horse collar!" the mother replied. She had nine fifty-cent pieces with her and she presented these with a promise to bring the rest next time she came to town. The husband returned, threw three silver dollars down on the counter, and went out with his family which now appeared at peace with the world. Abigail felt as if she had compounded a felony.

A few days later, she told the incident to a male merchant,

and asked him if she would ever receive the rest of her money.

"Of course," the storekeeper replied. "We merchants couldn't make any profit on fancy goods if it wasn't for what the women steal from their husbands."

Then sitting one night on the floor beside her husband's couch, Abigail related her experience in court. She had gone there with a woman friend, a widow. The county court had refused to accept the widow's annual statement as administratrix of her husband's estate. In fact the members of the court treated both women, the widow and Abigail, as if they were children.

"One-half the women are dolls, the rest of them are drudges, and we're all fools!" said Abigail when she had finished telling her husband of the experience.

"Don't you know it will never be any better for women until they have the right to vote?" Ben asked, patting her on the head.

"What good will that do?" demanded Abigail.

Ben explained patiently that since women do half the work in the world, besides bearing all the children, they ought to control half the pay. If they had the vote they would have just as much control over the lawmakers as the men.

"The light permeated the very marrow of my bones," said Abigail, "filling me with such hope, courage and determination as no obstacle could conquer and nothing but death could overcome."

Abigail decided the best way to spread this same hope and determination among other women of the Pacific Northwest was to start a newspaper. In 1871, the Duniways moved their family of one daughter and five sons to Portland, then a town of eight thousand people. Abigail rented a two-story frame house for forty dollars a month and set up her office and print shop in two upper bedrooms. A foreman, employed for twenty-five dollars a week, took charge of the mechanical department; he taught the growing Duniway boys how to set type and run the little press.

Abigail knew nothing about publishing a newspaper, and she was hesitant about consulting her brother. When the first issue of *The New Northwest* came out, however, her first caller was that august editor of *The Oregonian*. He complimented his sister highly on her paper, and though he would not openly espouse woman's suffrage, he reprinted articles from Abigail's little sheet and thus gave it welcome recognition. Soon women were reading *The New Northwest* throughout Oregon, Washington and Idaho.

For sixteen years the determined little woman and her five sons continued the publication. In its columns the women of the Northwest were exposed to arguments for women's rights. These were more or less subtly sandwiched between items of news, household and fashion hints and serial stories of pioneer life, nearly all written by Abigail herself.

She was no desk-bound editor either. Her items were written in ill-lighted hotel rooms, on river steamers, sometimes on swaying stagecoaches.

And she did not rely on the written word alone. She delivered the message of equal suffrage verbally, as well, wherever she could gather together a few people. Sometimes she spoke in churches, though in the early years they were usually closed to her. Not infrequently the back room of a saloon became her hall. And invariably she managed to sell subscriptions to *The New Northwest*.

Her career as a lecturer started the same year she became an editor. Susan B. Anthony, cruelly caricatured leader of the eastern feminist movement, came to Portland by steamer from San Francisco. Abigail was persuaded to become her manager and press agent during a two-month tour of Oregon and Washington. Her first introduction of the distinguished visitor in a little theater in Portland was so warmly received that from that time forward Abigail never lacked invitations to speak.

Miss Anthony, whom Abigail found to be a "most womanly woman" and not the man-hater she had been pictured, also was well received nearly everywhere. She and Abigail traveled by stage and steamer through the Willamette Valley, then north to Olympia, where they addressed the Washington Territorial Legislature, and on to Seattle and other cities on Puget Sound.

In Walla Walla they met their only serious rebuff. At Umatilla, their steamer had stopped for an hour, and Miss Anthony looked up the son of an old friend who lived in Rochester, New York. He turned out to be a barkeeper and tried to show his hospitality by offering Miss Anthony a glass of wine. She took a polite sip and returned the glass with a "thank you." Word of this indiscretion preceded the women to Walla Walla. Ministers there refused them the use of their churches. And since the Pixley sisters had engaged the only theater, the suffragists were compelled to speak in the dance hall of a saloon. The following Sunday they were denounced from the pulpits for having done so.

Because of all this controversy they were unable to organize a suffrage society in Walla Walla, as they had in many of the other cities. Still they received much publicity and were entertained by some of the "best" families. Being walloped in Walla Walla was very much like being banned in Boston.

"If you want any cause to prosper, just persecute it," commented Miss Anthony. Abigail remembered that truism to her dying day. She was often persecuted yet she always prospered.

There was the time, for instance, when a weekly paper was delivered to the Duniway home one Sunday morning. The family was seated at the breakfast table. Son Willis picked up the paper and turned to the editorial page. His face grew pale as he read a slanderous attack on the good name of his mother. He showed the paper to his older brother Hubert, and the two young men left the table, taking the paper with them. Sensing that something was wrong, Abigail followed them to the door begging them to do nothing rash. They did not reply, but hurried away. A short time later she was informed they had been arrested for assault and battery and released on bail furnished by a friend.

Next morning, when she left her house, the street was crowded with men excitedly discussing the affair. J. N. Dolph, later United States senator, crossed the street when he saw Abigail, lifted his hat and extended his hand. Then all the men in the crowd lifted their hats as she went weeping down the street.

The prosecuting attorney told Abigail later that as he arraigned her sons he had said to them in an aside: "Stay with it, boys. You did exactly right!"

Few women traveled alone in those days. Often Abigail was the only female in a stagecoach full of men. Whenever possible, she asked to sit over the "boot" beside the driver. There she was above the clouds of dust that rose from the rough dirt roads in summer and the mud that spattered from the ruts in winter. She was free, too, of the thick tobacco smoke filling the interior of the coach.

Often the editor-lecturer would take a stage following an evening meeting and ride on to the next town. After jolting over an unimproved road for an hour or two she would register at a small country hotel and probably be the only woman there. Sometimes a settler couple would take her

in, and then she might have to sleep in the same bed with two
or more small children.

Gossips spread lies about her. Wiseacres taunted her. But
Abigail gave as good as she got.

Prohibition of liquor was an important social issue of the
period. Though many ministers opposed woman's suffrage,
they endorsed the temperance movement. Abigail was in fact
a teetotaler, as were indeed her menfolk, but she held to the
belief that women who wished liberty for themselves should
not try to limit men's freedom of choice. She felt the prohibition movement, in which women were extremely active, worked
against equal suffrage, for many men believed that if the
women were permitted to vote they would immediately pass
laws prohibiting the sale and consumption of spirits. The
little editor was quite outspoken on the subject.

Nevertheless, she attended a meeting of prohibitionists in
Salem, since she too had once been active in the temperance
movement and still had many friends in it. As she entered the
church where the meeting was being conducted one of her
friends told her that at an earlier session a minister had
openly accused her of "indulging in Bacchanalian revelries
with men" in her hotel rooms. Abigail demanded the right to
reply to her accuser.

"I don't pretend to be a saint," she said. "I've done a good
many mean, little things I'm ashamed of in my life, but nobody knows about them but myself, and I won't tell. But,
suppose it were true that I had done the dreadful things of
which Mr. ———— has accused me, and nobody knows better
than my assailant that they are not true! But suppose they
were true! There are probably a hundred men in this assembly who have been drinking intoxicants today. Why doesn't
he bring their names before this body? Suppose that I, when
appearing before an Equal Suffrage convention, imagining

that Mr. ———— was absent, had dragged his name before the assembly, and repeated the often circulated scandal, falsely accusing him of killing four of his deceased wives!"

At the close of the session so many shook Abigail's hand that her shoulder became lame.

One time while riding on a stage in central Washington en route from Goldendale to Yakima and Ellensburg, the suffrage worker noticed that some men on the seat behind her were passing around a bottle. One of them became emboldened by the liquor and addressed Abigail in mocking tones.

"Madam," he said, "you ought to be at home, enjoying yourself, like my wife is doing. I want to bear all the hardships of life myself, and let her sit by the fire, toasting her footsies!"

It was almost dark, and snowing, when the coach reached Yakima. The driver went out of his way to drop the man at his own house. And there was his wife in the yard, chopping away at a snow-covered woodpile.

"I see, my friend, that your wife is toasting her footsies," said Abigail as her taunter descended from the coach. She heard later that the other men in the conveyance nicknamed him "Old Footsie Toaster."

Another time, a clever young bachelor, who was unalterably opposed to woman suffrage, debated Abigail on the subject. After holding forth for half an hour with stock arguments against votes for women, he concluded dramatically:

"I have often known a hen to try to crow, but I've never known one to succeed at it yet!"

Abigail's concluding statement convulsed the crowd with laughter.

"I once saw a rooster try to set, and he made a failure too," she said, mimicking her opponent's dramatic gestures.

When the suffragist attempted to speak at temperance meetings conducted in the basement of a Portland church, she found that a choir of hostile women had been organized against her. Whenever she rose to speak, the pastor would give a signal and the choir would burst into song and drown out her words.

Abigail solved the problem simply. During a lull in the meeting, she rose, raised her hand and said reverently, "Let us pray." The choir couldn't very well shout down a prayer.

She asked now that the Lord protect people from bigotry and tyranny of the pulpit as well as from the vice of the saloon; that press, people and pulpit be led to understand that absolute freedom for the female sex was the fundamental need of the awakening nation.

But at Jacksonville in the gold-mining region of southern Oregon the "arguments" and taunts against Abigail took solid form. There, in 1879, the little agitator was showered with eggs. She dismissed the throwers as "mostly old miners, or refugees from the bushwhacking regions of Missouri, whence they had been driven by the exigencies growing out of the Civil War."

A sheriff's posse had to be organized to protect her until she could ride the stage to other communities of southern Oregon's "fruit-laden hills and verdant vales" inhabited by "whole-souled men and hospitable women."

Jacksonville later became a center of support for the suffrage movement.

National recognition came early to the Northwest's foremost feminist. By 1871 she was already in demand as a lecturer in California. In 1872 she was a delegate to the annual convention of the National Woman Suffrage Association in New York. There she advocated the endorsement of Horace Greeley for President of the United States. But Susan Anthony, not sharing her faith in Greeley as a supporter of woman's suffrage, arranged that the northwesterner should be a member of a committee sent to interview the famous editor of the *New York Tribune.*

Greeley was cordial at first, but when Abigail asked his support of the suffrage movement his attitude changed.

"He brushed the fringe of his white whiskers under his smoothly shaven chin, and, speaking in a voice as hard as hail stones, said, 'I don't want women to be men!' " Abigail recalled in her memoirs.

"Neither do I," replied the doughty little woman. "I wouldn't be a man if I could! And now, Mr. Greeley, mark my words; you'll never be President! You'll find that women can tear down, if they are not permitted to build up."

In 1876, Abigail again traveled east to the Centennial Exposition in Philadelphia, at the invitation of Miss Anthony. The press received railroad passes in those days, and Harvey Scott was always glad to arrange free transportation for his sister. Expense money, however, was not so easy to obtain, and Abigail had only twenty-five dollars in her purse when she left Portland.

While bound up the Columbia River on a steamer, the editor of *The New Northwest* solicited subscriptions in the women's cabin. She confided the state of her finances to a woman passenger, and the latter obtained permission of the captain to hold a meeting for all passengers in the larger men's cabin. As the boat chugged between the sagebrush-covered hills east of the Cascades, Abigail lectured on her favorite subject. At the conclusion of her talk, the passengers took up a collection of eighty-seven dollars. At Wallula, she lectured again and received another contribution. At Walla Walla she added still further to her expense fund.

Abigail traveled by stage through Idaho and Nevada to reach the Union Pacific Railroad, which would take her east.

As usual she rode in her favorite spot beside the driver. At a way station, where they stopped for dinner, they found a lone woman stationkeeper mourning over her baby who had died just a few hours earlier. The grief-stricken woman had been waiting for the stage to take word to her husband who was working on railroad construction a dozen miles away. The hopeless sorrow of the lonely woman made a deep impression on Abigail.

"When I get to Heaven," she said to the driver after the stage got under way again, "I'm going to ask St. Peter to make me an usher so I can escort pioneer housewives and sturdy stage drivers to the highest seats!"

At the Philadelphia Exposition, Abigail again was impressed with the low position of woman:

"Compared with the great exhibits displayed elsewhere, in honor of the genus masculine, the women's 'show' was too meager to be otherwise than pitiful. After examining some dresses, sacred to royalty, and a few relics from the days of John Adams Sr., including the baby cap worn by John Quincy Adams Jr., when he was a week old, I wandered around to the end of the building, near which were stationed the different implements of warfare used by different nations. There were gatling guns, mounted howitzers, modern cannons, columbiads and other implements of destruction I cannot name, all with their muzzles pointed toward the Woman's Pavilion."

Early success came to the campaign for equal rights in the Pacific Northwest, though long years were to pass before final victory could be celebrated.

In 1874, the Oregon Legislature adopted a Married Woman's Property Bill giving a married woman the rights to her own business.

In 1883, the House of the Washington Territorial Legislature passed a woman's suffrage bill by a safe majority. Abigail was summoned to Olympia by her Washington co-workers to help persuade members of the Council, as the upper house was known, to pass the measure as well. She was the guest of Clara Sylvester, wife of the founder of Olympia, and paid her expenses by serving as correspondent for both her own weekly and for the *Portland Oregonian*. She sat nervously in the Council chamber as the "ayes" and "nays" were recorded on November 15. Only two other women were in the chamber. Her heart fairly stood still, she noted in her memoirs, when the final vote was cast giving women the vote by a majority of one.

The New Northwest had already gone to press in Portland, but when her sons received her jubilant telegram they opened the forms and gave Mom's big story the play it deserved. Soon newsboys were shouting in the streets. The little equal-suffrage paper was the first in the nation to print the news of the big victory for women.

Equal rights in Washington did not last, however. The prohibitionists became extremely active, and in 1886 a legislature elected by the help of the women's vote adopted a local option law. So when a constitution for the state of Washington was drawn up in 1887, women's suffrage was dropped.

Abigail, as we know, had foreseen the danger of mixing prohibition and woman's suffrage, but when the territorial legislature met in 1886 she could not answer the call to Olympia to fight for restraint. Her only daughter, Clara Bell, was on her deathbed in Portland. The daughter died on January 21 at the age of thirty-one.

Abigail was deeply attached to the one feminine member of her large family. As the daughter lay dying, the grieving mother bent over and whispered, "I wish I could go with you, darling!"

"You must stay to finish your work, Ma," her daughter replied.

Abigail did finish her work, even though for several years she was not as active as she had been. The family moved to Idaho in search of health for husband Ben and of income for the boys. They went into the cattle business.

But when sister fighters called for help, the aging leader came to their assistance. Once she traveled eighty miles by stage over dusty roads from the isolated Duniway ranch to the railroad at Blackfoot, where she caught the train to Boise. Her impassioned speeches helped make Idaho the first of the three Pacific Northwest states to adopt equal suffrage. That was in 1896, the same year Utah approved a similar provision.

Colorado had given women the vote in 1893. Wyoming women had voted since 1869; that state was not only the pioneer among states but among nations as well.

The Idaho victory, however, was marred for Abigail by the death, the same year, of her beloved and long-ailing husband.

Time and time again suffrage amendments were submitted to the voters in Oregon and Washington. Finally, in 1910, Washington voters approved. But that same year Oregon rejected a woman's-vote measure by 58,670 to 36,858. The indefatigable Abigail gathered her forces once more and on January 1, 1912, ordered the campaign to begin anew.

Governor Oswald West was one of the speakers in the Hall of Representatives in Salem when the kickoff meeting was held there in February. A College Equal Suffrage League was organized at the University of Oregon at Eugene. An automobile campaign was devised to send men and women to the outlying sections of Portland to speak from their cars. A suffrage float in the Rose Festival won first prize, and the silver cup was presented to Abigail on the front porch of her home, where she was now confined to an invalid's chair.

On October 22, the old lady's seventy-eighth birthday, a great gathering was held in the Gipsy Smith Auditorium. Gipsy Smith was an evangelist who held audiences spellbound much as Billy Graham does today. There was almost a religious fervor in the assembly as Abigail's wheelchair was carried to the platform for the climactic program of the campaign. This semireligious feeling was strengthened by the singing of a suffrage hymn written by the guest of honor herself. Speakers included, besides women prominent in the suffrage movement, the governor of Oregon, the mayor of Seattle, a former United States senator and other outstanding men.

Governor West brought the meeting to a warm and optimistic conclusion by inviting the little old woman in the wheelchair to write a women's "emancipation proclamation" as soon as the expected favorable vote had been counted.

On November 5, election day, campaign workers gathered in the Blue Room of the Oregon Hotel in Portland to await the returns. It was an exciting evening, for the vote was close. Abigail wasn't there. Before going home to bed, however, she had announced that if they were not successful, another campaign would be started immediately.

The amendment carried by a majority of 4161. The vote was 61,265 to 57,104.

Next day a reporter for *The Oregonian*, which this time had supported equal suffrage, found Abigail seated at home in a rocking chair, a pillow at her head, her spectacles in one hand while the other hand played idly with a bundle of letters and telegrams. She was not the least bit excited, the reporter said, simply peacefully contented.

Abigail wrote the emancipation proclamation, as the governor had asked her to. On December 2 the women of Oregon trooped to the polls for city elections. A woman even ran for mayor of Oregon City.

A historic photograph was taken in May, 1913, outside a polling place in Portland, the occasion being the first state-wide election in which women could vote. There are three women in the picture. Those standing at left and right are comparatively young, dressed in the mode of the day—suits with long skirts and coats that reach almost to the knee, blouses with high collars, and wide-brimmed hats. The woman in the middle is old, dressed in black with white gloves and with a black Windsorlike tie under her chin. On her head is a smallish black hat like grandmothers then wore. On her face is an enigmatic smile, such as Mona Lisa might have displayed in old age. The woman in the middle, of course, is Abigail Jane Scott Duniway.

Abigail died October 11, 1915, just eleven days before her eighty-first birthday. She is still remembered with admiration and respect by both men and women. All over the country, and virtually everywhere in the world, women enjoy the equal rights for which she fought so hard. The taunts she suffered are heard no longer, but her wise words bear repeating: "The struggle has never been a fight of woman against man, but always of broad-minded men and women on the one side against narrow-minded men and women on the other."

10 · NOAH KELLOGG—
LEGEND COME TO LIFE

This thriving town of Kellogg,
    'Bout sixty years ago,
Was just a wide space in the road,
    With none to come and go.

Then came a man with loaded pack,
    Noah Kellogg, so they say,
With all his goods upon a jack,
    Which he allowed to stray.

Next early morn he cast about
    To find his hobbled mule,
And though he hunted up and down,
    He could not find the fool.

At last he spied him on a ridge,
    And climbed up to him there.
The mule in flight kicked up a rock,
    Which looked almighty queer.

The story's long, it would, I fear,
    A ponderous volume fill—
Suffice to say the jackass found
    The famous Bunker Hill.

        —ANONYMOUS

The western legend of the old, gray-bearded prospector, trudging through the mountains with a mangy, mouse-colored burro at his heels, who strikes it rich at last on t'other side of yonder ridge, is not wholly fictitious.

Noah S. Kellogg was such a man. His burro was such an animal. And strike it rich they did!

Since the hot August day in 1885 when Mr. Kellogg—or was it his donkey?—stumbled upon the richest silver, lead and zinc lode in North America, hundreds of millions of dollars have come out of the mountains of northern Idaho. Nearby Spokane, Washington, metropolis of the "Inland Empire," owes much of its wealth and prosperity to old Mr. Kellogg—and his jackass.

Folklore of the Coeur d'Alene country may have given the jackass a bigger part than it deserved in the drama of the Bunker Hill and Sullivan mine discovery. The doggerel quoted above is but one of several versions told in the mining camps of Shoshone County in the past three quarters of a century. Miners, like all frontiersmen, believe a story worth telling is worth embellishing. Even the gray old prospector himself had his own version.

In any event, the jackass stole the show from the reserved old mystic, who even to his best friends was always *Mr.* Kellogg. True enough, a town was named for him. But otherwise he has retreated into the obscurity whence he came. A trail *and* a prairie, on the other hand, were named *Jackass.* To this day, the burro's picture is to be seen on calendars, paperweights and other objects throughout the region. Whether the oil painting of the jackass that hung in Dutch Jake's four-story Spokane saloon still exists is not known.

We are certain, however, that Noah, who was broke flatter than a prospector's flapjack, begged a pair of parsimonious old citizens of Murray, Idaho, to give him a grubstake. After much palaver they supplied seventeen dollars worth of grub and a three-dollar burro that the town deplored because of its loud, nocturnal braying. Old and rheumatic, ragged and depressed by years of failure, Kellogg must have been a sorry sight as he limped out of town under the hot, summer sun, the jackass following behind reluctantly. In a few days, however, he returned with a spring in his step and knowing where a fortune might be dug out of a mountain.

As one version has it, between the sad departure and the happy return, old Mr. Kellogg was plumb tuckered on his third night out. He tethered the jackass—not very carefully, it would appear—and lay down on his blankets to sleep. So much had been taken out of him by the hot sun and the difficult hike over fallen trees and rocks that he slept the clock around. When he awoke, the sun was high in the heavens. After he had stretched his aching muscles and cooked himself some coffee and bacon, the old man looked around for his donkey. It had slipped its tether and disappeared.

Nearly all day—so this story goes—the prospector scrambled through the brush, timber and boulders of Milo Gulch, looking for the critter. Finally, late in the afternoon, he heard it braying and then he saw it, grazing in a little meadow high on the mountainside. Noah picked his weary way to the animal and got a halter on it. More tired than ever, he sat down on a ledge to rest.

Idly, he picked up a loose rock and casually glanced at the spot where it had lain. His eyes popped! Suddenly his fatigue was gone! He had exposed what looked like the best galena— a rich ore of silver and lead—a man could expect to find anywhere. Noah sprang to his feet and with a few quick blows of his prospector's pick knocked off a few samples of the ore. Then casting his experienced eye over the terrain, he reached the joyous conclusion that the lode extended clear across the gulch. At his feet was a fortune!

This version of the discovery varies somewhat from the

one told in verse. Which, if either, is correct no one can say. Nobody in Kellogg, Wallace, Burke or Mullan will vouch for either. There seems to be some doubt also concerning Mr. Kellogg's own account, told somewhat sheepishly years later to Judge John R. McBride.

Yet Mr. Kellogg's story is the most intriguing and undoubtedly would be accepted without question if he, like most legendary old prospectors, had not been a bit balmy by most "practical" persons' criteria.

Noah had a vision of a great mountain of gold and silver lying in wait for him somewhere. The vision came to him first many years before as he lay on his cot in a miner's cabin in southern California. Whether he was asleep or awake when he got the mystic message he could not say. But there it was, in his gray, old head, sharp as a magic-lantern projection. It had led him to many places where gold and other valuable metals might be found, just as it had led him now up Milo Gulch on the South Fork of the Coeur d'Alene river in the panhandle of Idaho.

According to Kellogg, he and the burro were ascending a steep trail on that hot summer day in 1885. The jackass had been trained to follow its master like a puppy, but this day it held back. Thinking the donkey was just being obstinate, as its breed often is, the old man took hold of its halter and tried to lead it. When this failed, Noah got behind the beast and tried to drive it, but still the stubborn burro refused to budge.

Angered, the old man cut a willow switch from the side of the trail and applied it with vigor to the animal's rump. The jackass leaped forward a couple of paces, then planted itself firmly across the trail. Its head pointed toward a distant peak. Thus immobile from the head down, the critter opened its mouth and brayed, loud and long.

Noah could have been a little dizzy from the heat. Be that as it may, the sight of the stubborn burro, standing there braying and pointing with its long ears toward the mountain, reminded the prospector of a Biblical story. Balaam's ass must have looked much like that, the old man thought.

Mr. Kellogg was well versed in the Bible, as any man named Noah should be. He recalled the very words of Numbers XXII. 28:

"And the Lord opened the mouth of the ass, and she said unto Balaam, What have I done unto thee, that thou has smitten me these three times?"

Balaam's ass stubbornly had refused to move because it could see the Angel of the Lord barring the way with his sword. The ass could see what Balaam could not and thus saved her master's life by refusing to move.

Mr. Kellogg asked himself if his ass might not be trying to communicate in the same fashion as Balaam's. The vision of the mountain of gold and silver flashed through his mind, as it had so many times before. Could that be the visionary mountain the jackass was pointing to? It wouldn't hurt to find out, said the old prospector to himself, probably out loud. So he fought his way through more brush and fallen trees.

Sure enough! The mountain was virtually solid galena. Galena isn't gold, but it's worth a lot of money if found in such quality and quantity as this.

Thus, the Bunker Hill and Sullivan mine was discovered— if a visionary old man could be believed. The mine became the best producer of its kind in the country, if not in the world. Old man Kellogg's version takes a bit of faith to believe. But his own faith in a vision that paid off handsomely should make the intuitive donkey not too unbelievable.

Anyway, Kellogg did find the mine. And the jackass did

have a part in the discovery. A judge was to declare so officially!

Now few men have been as down on their luck for as long a time as was Noah Kellogg.

He was a wanderer, a jack-of-all-trades who failed at nearly everything he put his hand to. But he was naturally intelligent, with a well-developed bump of curiosity and a fair education. A contemporary said of him that his years of unrewarding pursuit of fortune on the rude frontier had not dulled his "refined nature." Years earlier he had mined in the Boise Basin of southern Idaho and later in northern Montana and in the Kootenay district of British Columbia. He was respected as one of the best prospectors in the West.

According to Judge McBride, who pumped the old man for his story and wrote it down, Mr. Kellogg was employed in 1873 as an attendant in the insane asylum at Steilacoom, Washington Territory. There he met a widow named Mrs. Byrd, who was a matron in the same institution. Kellogg was a confirmed bachelor of near fifty and, as mentioned earlier, was of an extremely reserved nature. Yet he fell in love with the widow and married her. The new Mrs. Kellogg's grown children did not take kindly to the romance.

Possibly the vision of the gold and silver mountain returned to Noah. In any event, he and his bride resigned their positions at the asylum not long after the wedding. The institution was not a likely place in which to find a fortune. But fortune eluded them elsewhere as well.

The couple moved often. Within a short period they lived at Tacoma, and at Nanaimo and Victoria, in British Columbia, where Mrs. Kellogg came down with a severe attack of asthma. Noah worked at odd jobs, cutting timber, clearing rights of way and digging ditches. A daughter of Mrs. Kellogg's, who had become reconciled with his stepfather, lived with them for a time. Mr. Kellogg developed rheumatism so severe he couldn't lift either foot more than six inches. The climate on the lower Columbia, where they lived for a time, and at Portland, where Noah ran a small saloon, was too damp, they decided, for both asthma and rheumatism. So they moved to Dayton in eastern Washington where the drier air might relieve their aches and wheezes. Noah bought a lot on credit there and built a small house of undressed lumber.

Then he went in debt for four yokes of oxen so he could bring logs from the Blue Mountains to a small sawmill in Dayton. He was doing pretty well as a logging contractor when a messenger arrived with word that Mrs. Kellogg had suffered a stroke. Kellogg hastened home and summoned two of his wife's daughters by telegraph. They came at once and one daughter remained to help look after her mother.

Noah, too, remained at his wife's bedside and as a consequence lost his business and his oxen. He was destitute now and in the spring decided he must look for work. Sadly he left his wife with the daughter, who agreed to care for the stricken woman. Mrs. Kellogg was too clouded of mind to realize that her husband was leaving.

For seven years, the aging, penniless man traveled through the West, often ill and without employment. On one occasion he sent home thirty dollars and on another the deeds to two lots he had bought at Medical Lake near Spokane. He ranged from the Canadian border to California. Somehow, though, his wanderings never took him to Dayton where his wife lay paralyzed in her rough-lumber shack.

He was in California when news broke of the discovery of gold in the Coeur d'Alene Mountains of Idaho. Noah's vision drove him north to join the rush of hopeful prospectors.

Mr. Kellogg had five dollars in the pockets of his well-worn clothes when he arrived at Eagle City in May, 1884. Borrowing sixteen dollars from a man named Garrison, he moved on to Murray. There was a big demand for lumber among the miners, and Noah bought a whipsaw with which he began laboriously sawing lumber by hand. Any prospect of profit vanished, however, when another man opened a water-power sawmill.

After digging ditches and doing carpentry, neither of which paid him well, Noah saw an opportunity to make some money splitting shingles. He obtained a used saw blade and made knives of it for his shingle mill. But, when the mill started, the knives flew to pieces. He was three hundred dollars in debt on this venture and never sold a shingle.

It was time to turn to the mountains again in pursuit of his vision.

The man Mr. Kellogg appealed to for a grubstake was a tall, gaunt, elderly New Englander named O. O. Peck. Peck was a small-time contractor for whom Kellogg had worked briefly. He was not of a mind to risk any money on the slim chance that Noah would find treasure in the hills. But when the old prospector pressed him, he put the proposition up to Dr. J. T. Cooper, an aging Scotsman who had been a surgeon in the British Navy. The Scotsman was no more inclined than Peck to throw money away. It appeared that Kellogg wouldn't get his grubstake.

Then, according to folklore, the legendary jackass brayed. It was a singularly penetrating bray, the kind with which the beast had kept the town of Murray awake through many a night. Peck and Cooper swore in exasperation. Canny old Noah perceived a new line of attack.

"Put a grubstake on that jackass's back and I'll take him out in the hills where he can't bother you," he told the parsimonious pair. That was the clinching argument. Dr. Cooper and Peck took Noah to Jim Wardner's store and charged seventeen dollars worth of provisions. These included thirty-five pounds of bacon, ten pounds of beans, fifteen pounds of flour and a small quantity of coffee and sugar.

The donkey set them back another three dollars. The animal had been abandoned at Murray by a miner from Colorado, but someone now laid claim to it, seeing an opportunity to get some money from the thrifty old men—a neat trick, indeed.

The old prospector set out with a mighty skimpy grub-stake. He reputedly mumbled in his beard about the stinginess of his benefactors as he trudged up the trail in the hot August sunshine. But probably his grubstakers wondered, as soon as the braying was muted by distance, what in tarnation had led them to gamble twenty dollars on the luck of such a luck-less old codger.

After the burro had re-enacted the role of Balaam's ass, the excited old man hastened back to Murray with his samples of ore. He was in such a hurry that he left the jackass behind. The contrary critter would only delay him. In Noah's head there was no "vision" at all of the great court battle that was to ensue.

At the mining camp, he testified later in court, he looked up Dr. Cooper and showed him the ore. He also asked the old Scotsman to buy him a meal, since he hadn't eaten all day. But Cooper was in an ugly humor. He was unimpressed with the galena, according to Kellogg, and refused even to buy him a dinner. The dour doctor virtually threw the ragged old prospector out the door.

"If that's the way you feel, I'm through with you!" Noah said he told his grubstake partner. This, he reckoned, was ample notice to both Cooper and Peck that their partnership was terminated.

Then he went to the saloon and gambling hall operated by Jacob "Dutch Jake" Goetz. The astute saloonkeeper recognized the value of the ore samples. He could distinguish aces from deuces in whatever form they might take. Dutch Jake set up a sumptuous meal for the tired and excited old man and got hold of Phil O'Rourke, who knew even more about ore. O'Rourke grew excited, too, when he saw the samples.

Jake bought supplies and provided horses, and Kellogg and O'Rourke set out for the mountain of galena, accompanied by another canny miner named Con Sullivan. There they posted claims on both sides of the gulch. O'Rourke suggested that one be called the Bunker Hill in honor of the knob in Boston where the famous battle was fought. The other was posted in Sullivan's name, though one story has it that it was named in honor of John L. Sullivan, the prizefighter.

Cooper and Peck, on the other hand, swore that Kellogg never came to either of them upon his return to Murray. Their lawyers insisted that Kellogg got to thinking it a shame to share his fortune with such stingy partners. So when he returned to Murray, he went straight to Goetz and O'Rourke instead of to his rightful partners, the lawyers charged, thus trying to cheat their clients of their legal shares.

William T. Stoll, junior counsel for Cooper and Peck, told their side of the dispute in a book published half a century later. Kellogg's original grubstakers first heard about the find several days after Kellogg, O'Rourke and Sullivan had posted the mine, Stoll asserted. They were naturally angry and hastened to the law office of Major W. W. Woods, with whom Stoll was associated. The lawyers agreed to represent them.

Stoll and a young prospector named John Flaherty headed for Milo Gulch to see what they could learn. There Flaherty happened upon a crumpled piece of paper which proved to be a claim notice signed by Kellogg. It bore the inscription: "N. S. Kellogg, ½; J. T. Cooper, ¼; O. O. Peck, ¼, locators."

This was evidence to the young lawyer that Kellogg had first posted the claims in his own name and that of his original partners, then had discarded these notices and substituted O'Rourke's and Sullivan's names, along with his own, on new postings.

The jackass entered the case again, as well. It turned out that Kellogg, in returning to the claims with his new partners, had picked up the burro along the trail, and it was with the group when the Kellogg-O'Rourke-Sullivan notices were posted. Some accounts of the litigation that followed relate that the judge took the donkey's presence into account in determining the case. The jackass virtually was declared a co-discoverer, and because it was the property of Cooper and Peck, they were entitled to profit by that fact.

Peck and Cooper's suit for a share in the mine went to trial the following June before Judge Norman Buck in the rude little courthouse at Murray, then the county seat of Shoshone County.

Everybody chewed tobacco, including the judge. Spittoons were considered effete, and there wasn't one in the whole room. When anyone had to spit, which was often, he aimed for a spot on the floor not occupied by human feet.

The benches outside the rail were filled to overflowing with interested miners, who, according to Stoll, were all for Kellogg, O'Rourke and Sullivan. No one liked Peck and Cooper, not even the lawyers who were pressing their case. And, besides, O'Rourke had been buying drinks all around for weeks.

W. H. Clagett, one of the attorneys for the Kellogg-O'Rourke-Sullivan combine, requested a jury to assist the judge in determining the facts, although in an equity case the judge was expected to make the final decision. The lawyer assured the judge that there was no question of his fairness and ability, but he argued that His Honor needed help in unscrambling the complicated case.

Everybody knew that a jury would find against Peck and Cooper, but Judge Buck aimed a stream of tobacco juice at a crack in the floor and allowed the motion.

Major Woods, in examining Noah, played on the old man's vanity. He complimented him on his newly attained affluence and respected position in the community. Then he led him into some dangerous admissions. One was that he couldn't have been starving when he returned to Murray and asked Cooper for a meal. He had been gone only a few days, the Major pointed out, and his grubstake of thirty-five pounds of bacon, ten pounds of beans, fifteen pounds of flour, and other provisions could not have been consumed in so short a time. Noah had to admit that there must have been quite a bit of grub left back at the claim.

The old prospector then was asked to write his name several times. The signature was compared with that on the scrap of paper Flaherty professed to have found which assigned quarter interests each to Peck and Cooper. Stoll declared there was no doubt that Kellogg had signed the crumpled claim notice.

Nevertheless, the jury deliberated only a few minutes and, as expected, decided against the ill-liked Peck and Cooper. Judge Buck was a fearless man, however. A few days later he delivered his decision contrary to the jury's findings and the sentiment of the community. He ruled that Peck and Cooper were entitled to share in the fortune.

The losers filed notice of appeal, but soon thereafter a Portland financier, Simeon G. Reed, appeared on the scene with an offer to buy the mine for something like a million dollars. The title had to be clear, however. The offer brought the antagonists together in a thrice. They would rather compromise, they decided, than lose an opportunity for all of them to become wealthy.

So they drew up an agreement giving Kellogg three hundred thousand dollars, O'Rourke two hundred thousand, Cooper and Peck seventy-six thousand, Sullivan seventy-five thousand and several others, who had a finger in the pie, lesser sums. The lawyers, of course, did rather well too. And Jim Wardner, who could smell opportunity for miles, got his share. He had had the foresight to file on the water rights in the stream above the Bunker Hill and Sullivan. These he sold to the new owners for a tidy sum, and got a contract, besides, for extracting great quantities of ore.

Discovery of the Bunker Hill and Sullivan lode brought prospectors by the hundreds into the Coeur d'Alene Mountains. Other good finds were made, and several mines went into production. By 1889 the Coeur d'Alene region was producing annually two and one half million dollars in metals, chiefly silver and lead. In 1890 the value was nearly five million. Ever since, rich metals have continued to pour out of the Idaho panhandle.

Daniel C. Corbin of Spokane built a narrow-gauge railroad to haul the ore from the mines to the head of navigation on the Coeur d'Alene River. There the ore was loaded on barges and hauled down the river, across Coeur d'Alene Lake and finally over the Northern Pacific Railway to Spokane. After that it was transhipped to smelters at Tacoma, Anaconda and elsewhere.

The little eastern Washington town, then known as Spokane Falls, grew in five years from about one thousand inhabitants to twenty-five thousand. Sawmills and flour mills sprang up along Spokane River, turning out lumber for the mines and mining towns and cereals for the miners' flapjacks. Men who had became wealthy from the mines retired to Spokane to invest their riches. They formed banks and many other businesses and built fine homes. Hotels, gambling establishments, saloons and other pleasure emporiums prospered.

"Dutch Jake" Goetz was one of the newly rich investors. He and his partner, Harry Baer, spent two hundred thousand dollars on a gambling and liquor palace. When, in 1889, fire swept Spokane, their place was destroyed with most of the other business houses. For a time they operated in a huge tent, then rebuilt lavishly. Down-and-out miners were permitted to sleep without charge in the basement. Gas and new-fangled electric lights illuminated the structure from first-floor saloon to fourth-floor dance hall.

Over the cherry-wood bar hung an oil painting of Noah Kellogg's jackass.

Sedate Mr. Kellogg did not spend his fortune in riotous living or for Spokane real estate. He stayed on in the little mining town that had been named for him.

The suit brought by Peck and Cooper and the negotiations for sale of the Bunker Hill and Sullivan delayed any return to him from his discovery. For months, he remained as penniless as he was the day he set out for Milo Gulch with the jackass.

Then at last he entered the office of Albert Allen, his attorney. The old man's face was troubled. He wished, he said, to confide in the lawyer a secret he had kept for years.

The old man told in detail of his marriage, of his long absence from his wife while he sought the fortune which shortly would be his.

"As soon as I receive the first payment from the sale," he

said, "I'll find her and devote my life and fortune in making her comfortable and happy."

Noah evidently was relieved to have told his secret. He left the lawyer's office in a happy frame of mind.

In a few days he returned, however, more distressed than before. He handed the attorney a letter and asked him to read it. The letter was from the daughter who had remained with Mrs. Kellogg when Noah left home so long ago.

Mrs. Kellogg was dead! She had succumbed to her lingering illness in July, 1886, nearly a year after her husband had made his lucky strike.

The daughter had read in the newspapers of the famous mine and Kellogg's connection with it. She told of her struggles through the years to care for her mother, always hoping that Noah would return to assist her. Now she was widowed and destitute. Wouldn't Kellogg please come to aid her?

The woebegone old prospector asked Allen if he would try to get an advance of one thousand dollars for him from the buyers of the mine. Allen went to Phil O'Rourke with the request. The latter, who had known Kellogg "like a brother" for several years, was astounded by the news that the shy, reserved old prospector had been married all that time. He wouldn't believe it until Noah confirmed it himself. Then he and Allen went with Kellogg to the cabin occupied by the agent of the mine purchasers.

It was a stormy evening. Heavy snow fell, driven by a bitterly cold wind. Yet, at the cabin door, the shy Kellogg would go no further. He remained outside while his friends entered to ask for the one thousand dollar advance. O'Rourke recalled later that he happened to glance through the window of the cabin. The light from the cabin lamp struck the face of the sad, old man waiting outside. The sight of tears streaming down the cheeks of the grief-stricken prospector made a deep impression on the warmhearted Irishman.

Kellogg got the thousand dollars and left immediately to find his wife's daughter, to help her financially and to hear more about his wife's long illness and death. When the sale finally was completed and Noah received the rest of his money, he spent many thousands on his wife's children. But, according to his acquaintances, the demands became exorbitant, and Kellogg finally had to refuse further payments to his stepchildren.

The daughter who had remained with Mrs. Kellogg brought action against the corporation which had purchased the Bunker Hill and Sullivan. The common-property laws of Idaho provided that if a husband abandoned his wife the whole of her estate should go, on her death, to the children, to the exclusion of the husband. So Mrs. Kellogg's daughter contended that Noah had abandoned his wife and that for this reason her children were entitled to her half interest in the share of the mine Noah had sold. The court found, however, that there was no proof Noah had abandoned his wife and that under the law he had a right to dispose of the property. The judge then sustained a motion by the defense for a nonsuit.

All litigation being finally concluded and his duties to his stepchildren performed to the degree he considered necessary, the old prospector lived a "retired life" in Kellogg. No longer did he have to climb over rocks and fallen trees to earn a grubstake. The vision had led him to a stake sufficient for the golden years—or galena years, perhaps, in his case. The "Mr." was now bestowed as a matter of course. Mr. Kellogg was an honored citizen of the city named for him.

Old Noah died on March 17, 1903. He lies in Greenwood Cemetery, on a knoll overlooking the mountain where he and a burro caught up with his inner vision.

What happened to the jackass is as shrouded in controversy as the part the critter played in the Bunker Hill and Sullivan discovery.

One account says that for a time the animal was a privileged character around Murray. But it continued to bray as loudly and long as it had before Mr. Kellogg took it on the legendary tramp through the mountains. Sleepless miners finally forgot the jackass's contribution to their well-being. So, one night, they lashed several sticks of dynamite to the burro's body, lit a long fuse, and prodded it into motion toward the outskirts of the town. As the jackass ran one way, the miners hurried in the opposite direction. Soon an explosion echoed through the canyon. The miners' sleep was not interrupted thereafter.

One historian wrote, however, that the donkey was rewarded with "a life of ease on a farm in Oregon." Since historians are usually more veracious than miners when it comes to storytelling, this account is probably the true one. At least one prefers to believe so.

11 · CHIEF JOSEPH —
NOBLE RED MAN

Old Chief Tu-eka-kas was deeply disturbed as he lay dying in his lodge in the Wallowa Valley of northeastern Oregon. White settlers were pressing in on the beautiful Land of the Winding Water. They desired the lush grass of the Wallowa Valley for their cattle, just as white miners had desired the gold in other Nez Perce territory on the Clearwater River in Idaho.

It was 1871, by the white man's reckoning, when Tu-eka-kas awaited the summons of Tah-Mah-Ne-Wes, the Great Spirit Chief above. As he lay there, the blind, frail old man thought ruefully of the long friendship between the Nez Perces and the fair-skinned ones who came from across the high mountains to the east.

That friendship began in 1805 when Meriwether Lewis and William Clark descended the trail from the buffalo country which runs through Lolo Pass. Since that day the blood of no white man had been spilled by a Nez Perce, not even that of French-Canadian trappers. These trappers had given the Indians the name by which white men generally knew them, and of which they were not fond. The trappers called them Pierced Noses because a few wore shell ornaments in their noses.

Now the old friendship was threatened. In 1855, Tu-eka-kas had put his X on a treaty with the white men's chiefs. Old Joseph, which was the Christian name bestowed on him by the Reverend Henry Spalding, was then assured that the Wallowa country would forever belong to his Wal-lam-wat-kin band of Nez Perces. But just eight years later, the invaders reneged on this promise. They presented a new treaty, reducing the Nez Perce land to one-sixth its original size. To be ceded to the white men's government was the Wallowa country, as well as lands occupied by several other bands.

Tu-eka-kas refused to sign this treaty of 1863. So did several other chiefs whose lands would be lost. But Chief Lawyer signed, for his band's ancestral grounds were retained within the smaller reservation. The white men now contended that Lawyer was head chief of all Nez Perces and that his signing committed all of them to move to the country surrounding Lapwai on the Clearwater River in Idaho.

For three years now the Indian agent at Lapwai had insisted that Old Joseph take his people across the Snake River and select land on the reservation. Tu-eka-kas and his eldest son, to whom he had delegated most of his duties, had so far ignored the agent's orders. They placed no trust in men who failed to live up to their promises. The friendship of so many moons was breaking up.

Already many Nez Perces, including Old Joseph's Wal-lam-wat-kins, had forsaken the white man's religion. The Book they had sought in St. Louis many years before had not shown the way to a better life. Now they followed the teachings of Smohalla, the "Dreamer," who preached that plowing the ground was the same as tearing the bosom of Mother Earth with a knife. To live off the land in its natural state was best for the Indian, he taught.

As Tu-eka-kas felt death approaching, he sent for Young Joseph, his son, whose Indian name was Hin-mut-too-yah-lat-kekht, "Thunder-rolling-in-the-mountains."

Young Joseph was thirty-one, six feet two inches tall, broad of shoulder and deep of chest. He carried his two hundred pounds with athletic grace. His chin was square and his eyes black and piercing. He wore his hair in two long braids over his shoulders.

The young chief knelt by his father's bed of furs and blankets and took the old one's hand in his.

"My son," said Tu-eka-kas in a failing voice, "my body is returning to my Mother Earth, and my spirit is going very soon to see the Great Spirit Chief. When I am gone, think of your country. You are the chief of these people. They look to you to guide them. Always remember that your father never sold his country. You must stop your ears whenever you are asked to sign a treaty selling your home. A few years more, and white men will be all around you. They have their eyes on this land. My son, never forget my dying words. This country holds your father's body. Never sell the bones of your father and mother."

Young Joseph pressed his father's hand and promised to protect his grave with his life. The old man smiled.

"I buried him in that beautiful valley of the winding waters," Young Joseph said several years later. "I love that land more than all the rest of the world. A man who would not love his father's grave is worse than a wild animal."

Only six years passed from the day Old Joseph died until Young Joseph had to choose between continued peace with the white men or war in defense of his homeland. He sought peace with patience and by compromise.

Chief Joseph's first attempt at peaceful settlement was temporarily successful. In March, 1873, he was summoned to Lapwai to meet with T. B. Odeneal, superintendent of Indian affairs for Oregon, and John B. Monteith, reservation agent. The white officials informed him they had orders from the Great White Chief that all Nez Perces must be settled at Lapwai. The government would help him in many ways if he obeyed these instructions, they said. Joseph must have smiled wryly at this. The government had promised the treaty Indians many things, few of which had been delivered.

"I did not want to come to this council," the tall young chief replied, "but I came hoping that we could save blood. The white man has no right to come here and take our country. We have never accepted any presents from the government. Neither Lawyer nor any other chief had authority to sell this land. It has always belonged to my people. It came unclouded to them from our fathers, and we will defend this land as long as a drop of Indian blood warms the hearts of our men."

Odeneal and Monteith decided Joseph was right. On their recommendation, President Grant withdrew the Wallowa Valley from the public domain. But Governor L. F. Grover of Oregon, under pressure from white settlers, protested the order. A government commission in 1876 ruled for the settlers, and again Joseph's people were ordered to move from the Land of the Winding Water. Another act of white man's perfidy had strained the friendship Joseph's grandfather had pledged to Lewis and Clark.

Meanwhile, trouble brewed in the Wallowa country between the white settlers and the Indians. The whites complained that Joseph's men had driven off and killed stock and threatened the settlers. Agent Monteith found these complaints untrue.

The trouble reached a climax when A. B. Findley and Wells McNall went looking for some horses they thought the Indians had stolen, but which were found later grazing near the Findley ranch. The white men were armed with rifles. At the Nez Perce village they were met by a group of Indians who resented the accusation that they were thieves. The settlers and the braves got into a heated argument. McNall pointed his gun at the Indians and one of them, We-lot-yah, tried to wrest it from him. McNall called to Findley to help him. The latter fired and We-lot-yah was killed. Agent Monteith reported the shooting was "willful, deliberate murder."

Joseph issued an ultimatum to the settlers to surrender the murderers or he would destroy their farms. Troops were sent in from Walla Walla. A battle was averted when Joseph, in a parley with Lieutenant Albert G. Forse, agreed to keep his men south of Hurricane Creek if the whites remained on the north side.

The slayers of We-lot-yah were then tried at Union and a jury of ranchers acquitted them.

Still another commission recommended that Joseph's band be moved to Lapwai, and in January, 1877, the Department of Interior issued orders to Monteith to see that this was done.

Monteith sent Head Chief Reuben, Joseph's brother-in-law; James Reuben, the latter's son; Whisk-tasket, Joseph's father-in-law; and Captain John, a Nez Perce scout, from Lapwai to Wallowa to inform Joseph of the edict. The reservation Indians argued that reservation life had many advantages and that Joseph should select land near Lapwai before other non-treaty Indians picked the best tracts. Joseph meditated on the order overnight. Then he spoke:

"I have been talking to the whites many years about the land in question, and it is strange they cannot understand me. The country they claim belonged to my father, and when he died it was given to me and my people, and I will not leave it until I am compelled to."

The next move of the whites was to compel him.

In April, General Oliver O. Howard, one-armed veteran of the Civil War and now commander of the Department of the Columbia with headquarters at Vancouver, traveled by steamer and other conveyances to Lapwai for a council with all the nontreaty chiefs. Besides Joseph, these Indian leaders were Looking Glass, whose band lived on Clear Creek near the Middle Fork of the Clearwater River; White Bird, whose people lived on the Salmon River; Hush-hush-cute, chief of a band from the Asotin country of southeastern Washington; and Tuhulhutsut, whose Snake River group was small but whose influence on the other nontreaty Nez Perces was great. Tuhulhutsut was a leading *tewat,* or medicine man, of the Dreamer religion, known for his inflammatory oratory. None of these chiefs were as impressive physically as either Joseph or Alokut, Joseph's brother, who was even taller than he.

General Howard's mission was to tell the nontreaty Indians to move at once to the reservation—or else.

On the parade ground at Fort Lapwai a large hospital tent was set up, its sidewalls stretched out like awnings. Here the council would be held.

On the morning of the parley, the Indians donned their best tribal costumes. The men's hair was carefully braided and tied with colored cloth. Bright blankets were thrown over their shoulders. The women were as gaily garbed in bright shawls, blankets and skirts decorated with shells and elks' teeth.

On painted ponies, fifty warriors rode in single file to the fort where General Howard, Agent Monteith and Perrin Whitman, nephew of the martyred missionary Marcus Whitman, waited. Young Whitman was to serve as interpreter. The women followed in their high-pommeled saddles.

The Indians chanted a shrill, weird song as they rode around the fort before dismounting and entering the tent. There they shook hands with General Howard and his aides, then sat down on the ground in circles with the head chiefs in the front circle.

General Howard had ordered the troops at the fort to remain in their barracks during the talks, ready for any emergency. Meanwhile, by his orders, cavalry units were moving into the Wallowa country and to Lewiston, Idaho. News of this aroused suspicion and resentment among the chiefs.

Tuhulhutsut delivered a highly critical speech when the assembled chiefs rose to answer General Howard's explanation of the order from Washington. There was nothing in the Dreamer faith, the *tewat* declared, saying that white men could dictate where red men should live:

"The Great Spirit Chief made the world as it is, and as he wanted it, and he made a part of it for us to live upon. I do not see where you get your authority to say that we shall not live where he placed us."

When General Howard admonished him for arousing the Indians and threatened to place him in the guardhouse if he continued, the medicine man demanded:

"Who are you that you ask us to talk, and then tell me I shan't talk? Are you the Great Spirit? Did you make the world? Did you make the sun? Did you make the rivers to run for us to drink? Did you make the grass to grow? Did you make all these things, that you talk to us as though we were boys? If you did, then you have the right to talk as you do."

Tuhulhutsut was placed in the guardhouse.

Thus was another link forged in the chain of war. The medicine man would never forget the disgrace of physical confinement at the hands of an officer of a government which had no right to say where he should live.

Still the man of peace, Joseph counseled the angry warriors against using the knives they carried under their blankets.

"The arrest of Tuhulhutsut was wrong," he told the Indians, "but we will not resent the insult. We were invited to this council to express our hearts, and we have done so."

General Howard gave the nontreaty bands thirty days in which to move to the reservation. Joseph protested this was not long enough to round up his people's horses and cattle and ford them across the swollen Snake River. But the general was adamant. Chief Joseph went sadly back to the Wallowas to attempt the impossible.

Many of his young men were willing to fight rather than "be driven like dogs from the land where they were born." Joseph urged them not to resist.

"I said in my heart that rather than have war I would give up my country," he recalled. "I would give up my father's grave. I would give up everything rather than have the blood of white men upon the hands of my people."

At the Snake River, women and children were ferried across on buffalo-skin rafts, with a mounted horse at each corner of the frail craft. Then part of the stock was driven into the swift-flowing stream. A cloudburst in the midst of this operation swept many horses and cattle to their death. Joseph ordered that the remaining cattle be kept on the Oregon shore until the river subsided. There white men attacked his guards and stole the animals. The patience of an extremely patient man was sorely tried.

Joseph did not take his people directly to the reservation. They had eleven days until the deadline. These they decided to spend at White Bird's camp in Rocky Canyon by the Salmon River eight miles west of Grangeville. The other nontreaty bands were there also.

Bitter words were spoken against the white men. Tuhulhutsut demanded war to wipe out the disgrace of his confinement. Many of the young men pleaded for an opportunity to avenge the wrongs they and their families had suffered. But Joseph, though accused of cowardice by some of the medicine men, insisted on peace.

Perhaps the peace would not have been broken if Joseph

had not been preoccupied by the imminent birth of a child to one of his two wives and by the need to butcher beef for his family. While he was absent from the council, some of the young men became inflamed with whisky they bought from white settlers. One of them, Walaitits, a White Bird Indian, whose father had been killed by a white man, was taunted by an old man.

"If you are so brave, why do you not avenge the murder of your father?" the old one yelled at him as he rode through camp.

The young Indian accepted the challenge. Two other young warriors, Isapsis-ilpilp and Um-til-ilp-cown, also members of White Bird's band, set off with him on their horses for Slate Creek, murder in their hearts. There they slew Richard Divine, a retired sailor. Next day they killed three other settlers and wounded another. On June 14 they rode back into camp with the settlers' guns and horses.

Blood lust now ran wild among many of the Indians. Tuhulhutsut and seventeen warriors joined the three original raiders on another foray during which several settlers were killed or wounded.

Some of the Indians, wishing to avoid war, left the camp, either for Lapwai or other campsites. They advised Joseph to do likewise.

"I can't go back," said Joseph. "The white people will blame me."

"I was deeply grieved," the chief was to recall. "I knew that their acts would involve all my people. I saw that the war could not be prevented. I counseled peace from the beginning. I knew that we were too weak to fight the United States. We had many grievances, but I knew that war would bring more. . . . I would have given my own life if I could have undone the killing of white men by my people."

War was not long in coming. Governor Mason Brayman of Idaho Territory issued guns and ammunition to settlers of the part of Idaho threatened by the uprising. Volunteer companies were organized in several small, pioneer settlements. Colonel David Perry, commander of Fort Lapwai, was sent by General Howard with Troops F and H of the First Cavalry, ninety-nine men in all, to protect the people of Grangeville and Mount Idaho. Captain Joel G. Trimble and Lieutenants William R. Parnell and Edward R. Theller of the Twenty-first Infantry were assigned to Perry to assist him.

The atrocities continued. When Colonel Perry's men reached Grangeville at nightfall of June 16 they were met by excited, angry townspeople. The Indians had been seen that day headed for White Bird Canyon. The settlers urged Perry to attack them there at once, lest they cross the Salmon River and escape.

"They're cowards!" said one settler. "We could lick them ourselves if we had enough guns and ammunition!"

Colonel Perry took the advice. His troopers, tired from a seventy-mile ride, remounted. It was sixteen miles from Grangeville to the canyon where the Indian camp lay. As the soldiers approached the head of White Bird Canyon, one of them struck a match to light his pipe. An Indian posted as guard saw it and gave warning with a piercing howl like that of a coyote.

The soldiers rested on the plateau at the head of the canyon for the short time remaining until daybreak. Then they rode down the steep canyon to where the Indian camp supposedly was concealed behind a knoll. But Joseph, having been warned by the coyote howl, was ready for them. He sent White Bird with a group of warriors to the left of the cavalry's line, Alokut to the right.

A small group of white volunteers who had been assigned

to hold a knoll were driven from it. Indians seized the high ground and poured enfilading fire into the bluecoats. Other warriors sent a herd of horses through the soldiers' line, Indians clinging to the horses' sides. Soon they were firing from the rear as well as from the flanks.

Perry's troops, many of them new recruits, broke under the vicious attack. The commander ordered a retreat to ridges in the rear. Lieutenant Theller and eighteen men were driven into a ravine against a steep bluff. For them there was no escape. They fought to the last man and the last cartridge. Not one survived.

Joseph's warriors pursued the soldiers hotly. Four miles from Mount Idaho, civilians came to the aid of the troopers. Then the Indians disappeared, as if into the ground.

Thirty-three bluecoats died in the battle, one-third of the men in action. Joseph's casualties were believed to be four wounded. Sixty Indians had routed one hundred trained soldiers and nearly annihilated them. Only the Custer massacre in 1876 was more disastrous to white troops engaged in war with Indians. No one would say again that the Nez Perces were cowards. Their discipline was far superior to the whites'. Their war chief had proved himself a master tactician.

A daughter was born to Joseph's wife during the battle. This happy fact did not relieve his sadness over the outbreak of war. But the other Nez Perces danced and whooped to the savage beat of the *tewats'* drums.

The next encounter was between Joseph and General Howard, himself. Calling on troops from widely scattered parts of the Northwest and on volunteers, the one-armed general marched on the Nez Perce camp with 580 men, hoping to avenge Perry's defeat.

But the tall Indian tactician played hide-and-seek. Joseph

took his people across the Salmon River to the safety of the forested mountains. Howard pursued him, crossing with much more difficulty than had the Indians.

Joseph now had several avenues open to him. He could move west, ford the Snake and return to his own Wallowa country. He could cross the Salmon again and attack the white troops from the rear. He could hide in the Seven Devils country. Or he could strike toward the east to the Lolo Pass trail and the buffalo country.

Joseph crossed the Salmon. His warriors harassed Howard's forces from the rear in bloody encounters. Finally the white and red forces came to grips on the Clearwater.

Joseph now boasted some three hundred warriors, having been reinforced by Looking Glass and his band and by other Nez Perces who were impressed by his victory at White Bird Canyon. But Joseph had to retreat now before the superior white forces. His losses were heavier this time than Howard's. Twenty-three of his warriors were killed and more than thirty wounded; the white men lost thirteen men and had thirty wounded.

Yet Joseph's people were still free. They had fought to a standstill a force of supposedly well-trained soldiers of twice their own number. General Howard, on the other hand, felt that, even though he had not captured or annihilated the Nez Perces, he had at least stopped the murders and freed Idaho from peril. Still, this general who had helped plan the battle of Gettysburg said, "I do not think that I had to exercise more thorough generalship during the Civil War than I did in the march to the battlefield and the ensuing battle with Joseph and his Indians on the banks of the Clearwater."

The Nez Perces retreated eastward to Kamiah and Howard's troops followed. But Howard was delayed in attacking again by a messenger from Joseph, who, under a flag of truce, asked his terms for surrender. Unconditional, was Howard's reply. Meanwhile the Nez Perces moved up the trail to a position they could defend indefinitely.

Now the Indians had to decide what to do next. Should they flee eastward into the Bitter Root Valley on the Montana border and give up any claim to their own land? Should they fight it out at this point? Or should they accept the surrender terms? The chiefs, called into council by War Chief Joseph, were divided. Go to the buffalo country, said one. Seek aid from the Crows or the Shoshones, said another. Go where Sitting Bull is (Canada), advised a third.

Joseph vehemently opposed further flight.

"What are we fighting for?" he asked. "Is it for our lives? No! It is for this land where the bones of our fathers are buried. I do not want to take my women among strangers. I do not want to die in a strange land. Some of you tried to say, once, that I was afraid of the whites. Stay here with me now, and you shall have plenty of fighting. We will put our women behind us in these mountains, and die on our own land fighting for them. I would rather do that than run I know not where."

But the others—even Tuhulhutsut—were tired of fighting. They outvoted their war chief. And so Joseph began, reluctantly, a masterly retreat covering some eighteen hundred miles in distance and two and one half months in time.

The Nez Perces moved leisurely up the Lolo Trail, gathering food as they went. Howard followed, but with difficulty. The general wired the military authorities at Missoula, Montana, asking them to block the eastern end of the trail until he could catch up with Joseph.

Captain Charles C. Rawn was sent with forty regulars and one hundred volunteers from the Bitter Root Valley. The white men built a barricade at the mouth of the trail. When the Nez Perces arrived they asked for a parley with Rawn and his officers. They would harm no settlers in Montana nor attack the white troops if they were allowed to pass, Joseph declared. All they wished was to reach the buffalo country and find a new home.

The volunteers favored making a deal with Joseph; they did not wish their homesteads burned or their families injured. But Rawn could not disobey his orders. For two days, at noon, the parleys were held. On the third day at dawn Rawn decided to attack.

As he prepared to move forward, the officer heard singing on the mountainside above the barricade. Looking up, he saw the rear guard of Joseph's band passing into a canyon. Between talks the chief had surveyed the land and had discovered a way to bypass the fortifications which soon became known among the frontiersmen as "Fort Fizzle."

The Indians relaxed their guard after passing safely through Lolo Pass. At a place called Big Hole they camped to rest, fish in the clear waters of Ruby Creek, cut lodgepole pine for use in the treeless buffalo country, and hunt antelope and other game. Joseph did not know that Colonel John Gibbon with 146 men of the Seventh Infantry and thirty-four civilian volunteers had been dispatched, on telegraphic request from Howard, to intercept the Nez Perces. On August 8, the white troops came upon the unguarded Indian camp. They were undetected and concealed themselves successfully.

Next morning at dawn the white troops attacked the Indian encampment. The Nez Perces were taken completely by surprise. The soldiers, yelling like savages, rushed into the village and fired point-blank at naked braves who dashed from their lodges with sleep-laden eyes. Women and children screamed, dogs barked and horses neighed. The Indians headed for the river and the willows growing there. Joseph rallied his warriors, and they laid down a heavy fire on the invaders.

Two white officers were killed. Their men were aroused to a blind fury and began clubbing all Indians within reach, women and children as well as men. They attempted to burn the lodges, but the skin tepees were wet with heavy dew and would not ignite. Still some of the Indian possessions flared up as the torch was put to them. The sight of their burning camp gave renewed vigor to the Indian counterattack.

Looking Glass was heard calling the names of the three Indians who had started the war by murdering the Idaho settlers.

"This is battle!" he shouted. "These men are not asleep as those you murdered in Idaho. . . . Now is the time to show your courage and fight!"

Two of the three braves died that day. The third was killed in a later skirmish.

Nonetheless the Nez Perces finally turned the tables on the white soldiers. They drove the whites from the camp and surrounded them in the timber. Then under fire of the soldiers, the Indians reoccupied their village. Squaws, wailing with grief and horror at the sight of the carnage, pulled down the tepees and loaded them and other possessions on their ponies. Then they fled down the valley with the children.

General Howard came up at this point, possibly saving Colonel Gibbon's command from the same fate that befell Custer on the Little Big Horn. Joseph withdrew his forces, leaving nineteen warriors and seventy women and children dead on the battlefield. Thirty-one white soldiers were killed and thirty-eight wounded. Many more Indians died from wounds as they fled from the field. Joseph admitted later that 208 of his people perished as the result of the Big Hole fight.

This was a hard blow. But the Nez Perces—at least those who survived—still were free.

There followed a long pursuit of the Nez Perces by General Howard. Joseph took his people back into Idaho, possibly hoping to return to his beloved Land of the Winding Waters. But, when the Shoshones refused to join him, he turned east again into Montana. Reports came to Howard that the Indians were pillaging ranches they passed. Eight men were killed on a ranch at Horse Prairie Creek. Some historians attribute this wanton destruction to Indian anger at the slaying of women and children at Big Hole.

Southeast and east rode Joseph's people, pursued by Howard, through Yellowstone Park, then north across the Yellowstone, Musselshell and Missouri rivers toward Canada. Several skirmishes were fought with troops sent out to intercept them, the last at Cow Creek Canyon in north central Montana, where Joseph's rear guard drove off a company of volunteers under Major Guido Ilges.

Joseph felt secure now. The Nez Perces moved leisurely over the plateau country, where bunch grass provided sustenance for his horses. But he was to make a fatal mistake, perhaps because of a false sense of security.

On the northern slopes of the Bearpaw Mountains, within one day's march of the Canadian border, the war chief called a halt. Hunting was good there, and his people and horses needed to rest and recuperate from their wounds.

"I sat down in a fat and beautiful country," Joseph said in an interview in 1900. "I had won my freedom and the freedom of my people. There were many empty places in the lodges and in the council, but we were in the land where we would not be forced to live in a place we did not want. I believed that if I could remain safe at a distance and talk straight to the men that would be sent by the Great Father, I could get back the Wallowa Valley and return in peace."

But he was not yet in the land of the redcoats, and he did not adequately scout the country about him!

The one-armed hero of the Civil War had set a trap for his wily Nez Perce opponent. In his long chase of Joseph, General Howard had discovered that the chief kept one day's march ahead of the bluecoats. When Howard speeded up, so did Joseph. When Howard slowed his march, so did the war chief.

Now the general purposely delayed his advance to stop Joseph from hurrying into Canada. Then he sent a written order by boat down the Yellowstone to Colonel Nelson A. Miles, directing Miles to proceed in a northwesterly direction from what was later named Fort Keogh and intercept the Indians south of the Canadian border. Miles started out on September 17 with three troops of the Second Cavalry, three troops of the Seventh Cavalry, four companies of the Fifth Infantry mounted and two unmounted companies of the Fifth Infantry, guarding a wagon train. He also had a Napoleon cannon and a breech-loading Hotchkiss gun.

Colonel Miles kept the Little Rockies range between him and the Nez Perces and sent Cheyenne scouts to the ridges to spy on Joseph's band. At eight o'clock on the morning of September 30 the cavalry reached the village and charged over a rise into the camp.

However, the Indians were not completely surprised. A Nez Perce boy, who had gone out to tend his pony, had seen the Cheyenne scouts and had warned the chiefs. Many of the warriors had time to take up positions in the trenches they had learned since Big Hole to dig. They held their fire until the troopers were within one hundred yards. Then they delivered such a withering volley that the soldiers had to retreat.

The Nez Perces had learned to identify the officers by their spoken commands and directed their fire especially at them. Only one officer of the Seventh Cavalry was unwounded after the first charge, and of the 115 men in the battalion, fifty-three were killed or wounded.

Joseph also lost outstanding commanders. Killed that first day were Looking Glass, Tuhulhutsut and Joseph's brother Alokut.

Some Nez Perce women and children, defended by a small group of warriors, were cut off from the main camp in the attack. They escaped, probably to Canada.

"We had no knowledge of Miles' army until a short time before he made a charge upon us, cutting our camp in two and capturing nearly all of our horses," recounted Joseph. "About seventy men, myself among them, were cut off. My little daughter, twelve years of age, was with me. I gave her a rope, and told her to catch a horse and join the others who were cut off from camp. I have not seen her since [this was in 1879], but I have learned that she is alive and well.

"I thought of my wife and children, who were now surrounded by soldiers, and I resolved to go to them or die. With a prayer in my mouth to the Great Spirit Chief who rules above, I dashed unarmed through the line of soldiers. It seemed to me that there were guns on every side, before and behind me. My clothes were cut to pieces and my horse was wounded, but I was not hurt. As I reached the door of my lodge, my wife handed me my rifle, saying: 'Here's your gun. Fight!' "

Subsequent charges by Miles' troops failed to dislodge the entrenched Indians. At night, a blizzard blew up, causing severe discomfort to both sides. The colonel, who was soon to become a general, laid a siege to the camp that lasted for five days. Joseph sent messengers through the lines in an attempt to reach Sitting Bull in Canada and to persuade him to bring his Sioux warriors to his aid. But Sitting Bull's band withdrew farther into the redcoat country, instead.

It was still snowing when General Howard arrived at Miles' camp on the evening of October 4. Miles had already begun negotiations with Joseph, seeking his surrender. Howard told him to continue to parley. He would not take over command until after Joseph had given himself up, the general declared, and Miles would receive credit for capturing the Indians!

Howard's Nez Perce scouts, Captain John and Old George, were sent to negotiate with Joseph. The war chief understood from these men that Miles promised they could return to their own country with the stock they had left, if they surrendered now.

Captain John delivered Joseph's dramatic reply to the white officers. It was taken down verbatim by Lieutenant C. E. S. Wood of the Twenty-first Infantry, Howard's acting adjutant general.

"Tell General Howard I know his heart," was Joseph's message. "What he told me before I have in my heart. I am tired of fighting. Our chiefs are killed. Looking Glass is dead. Tuhulhutsut is dead. The old men are all dead. It is the young men who say yes or no. He who led the young men [Alokut] is dead. It is cold and we have no blankets. The little children are freezing to death. My people, some of them, have run away to the hills, and have no blankets, no food; no one knows where they are—perhaps freezing to death. I want to have time to look for my children and see how many of them I can find. Maybe I shall find them among the dead. Hear me, my chiefs. I am tired; my heart is sick and sad. From where the sun now stands I will fight no more forever."

At 4:00 P.M. on October 5, Joseph rode to Miles' camp, accompanied by a guard of five warriors. His clothes bore more than a dozen bullet holes and his head and one wrist showed scratches made by bullets. The war chief's head was bowed as he rode up the slight rise to where the white officers stood. As he reached them he straightened and swung off his horse. Stretching out his arm, he offered his rifle to General Howard. The general motioned toward Colonel Miles, and the latter accepted the weapon. Then Joseph shook hands with his captors in solemn dignity, turned on his heel and entered a tent provided for him.

White Bird and 104 of his band escaped that night and joined Sitting Bull in Canada. Eighty-seven warriors, of whom forty were wounded, surrendered with Joseph. Also placed in Miles' custody were 184 women and 147 children.

Eighteen Indians had been killed in the final battle. Twenty per cent of the greatly superior white force were casualties. In the long campaign, Joseph had engaged some two thousand soldiers with no more than three hundred fifty warriors at any time. Losses of the whites totaled 126 killed and 140 wounded. Joseph's losses were 151 killed and eighty-eight wounded, besides women and children whose number in dead and wounded is unknown.

Never had a commander, untrained in modern warfare, fought so brilliantly against highly trained officers and men. He deserved the respect now universally accorded him.

Thunder-rolling-in-the-mountains was not yet done with white men's faithlessness.

It was too late that year to transport his people across the mountains to Lapwai. Howard and Miles decided to keep them at Fort Keogh until spring, then escort them back to their own country.

But higher authorities in Washington, as usual, saw no reason to live up to the promises of their representatives in the field. Instead of following the recommendations of General

Howard and Colonel Miles, the War Department ordered the Nez Perces removed first to Bismarck, North Dakota, and later to Leavenworth, Kansas. There many of the Nez Perces sickened and died of malaria.

A few months later the survivors were sent to Indian Territory, now in Oklahoma. They did not thrive there, in country so different from their own land of cold streams and forested mountains.

In 1879, Joseph was permitted to go to Washington to lay his case before President Hayes and Congress. It earned him nothing except more broken promises.

Not until the spring of 1885 were Joseph's people allowed to return to the Pacific Northwest. Only 268 men, women and children remained in the band. They made the homeward journey by rail, in sharp contrast to their fighting retreat to exile on horseback.

Joseph was to suffer still more for a war he didn't wish to fight. At Pocatello, Idaho, the Nez Perces were divided into two groups. One group, of 118 persons, was taken under military escort to Lapwai. The other group, of 150, Joseph included, was taken to the Colville Reservation in northeastern Washington. It wasn't safe, white authorities held, for Joseph to settle among whites who had lost members of their families in the conflict.

The noble red man was not forgotten, however. In defeat, he was honored by his conquerors. In 1897 he went to New York for the dedication of Grant's tomb. He was a guest of Buffalo Bill and rode in the parade. In 1904 he and General Howard sat side by side at commencement exercises at Carlisle Indian School in Pennsylvania.

In 1903 he went to Washington to ask President Theodore Roosevelt to give the Wallowa Valley back to his people. He also visited Portland and Seattle, always emphasizing his desire to lead his band back to their homeland.

Joseph's most poignant journey from the reservation where the white men said he must live came in June and July, 1900. Indian Inspector James McLaughlin, who had been directed to investigate the possibility of restoring part of the Wallowa Valley to the Nez Perces, took the graying chief to his beloved homeland. Joseph found his father's grave enclosed by a fence erected by a white friend. The old man wept.

Yet despite this heart-rending journey, McLaughlin recommended against returning the Nez Perces to the Wallowa country. This removed the old chief's last hope. When the word came to him, in 1904, he took to sitting whole days before his fire, silent and unmoving. On September 21, 1904, he fell forward toward the fire and died.

A monument stands at Joseph's grave at Nespelem on the reservation where he did not wish to live. Twenty-one years after his death, one hundred of his people were permitted to return to his homeland to dig up the bones of his father and carry them to the shore of Wallowa Lake. There the remains were reinterred beneath a granite column, while two thousand white persons looked on respectfully. A town in the Wallowa country is named Joseph. All over the Northwest his memory is revered.

But the white men still own the Land on the Winding Water, a land which Joseph's band never sold. The honors bestowed on Joseph in his late years and since his death cannot atone for the deceit, the broken promises, the bloody war forced upon him during his lifetime. Who was the savage and who the civilized in the white men's conquest of the red men's America? In the case of Chief Joseph, the answer is obvious.

12 · JIM O'SULLIVAN —
BULLDOG OF GRAND COULEE

It was hot in the hamlet of Ephrata, Washington, even under the shade trees which set it apart from neighboring towns. Miniature dust-devils skittered along the dirt street.

Short, chunky Billy Clapp, amiable, fortyish lawyer, got out of the sun as soon as he could. He stepped into a small restaurant, wiping his brow on his shirtsleeve. Inside he found Paul Donaldson, a young mining prospector. They fell into conversation over coffee and doughnuts.

Donaldson had just returned from Grand Coulee, where he had been exploring for mineral deposits. He and Clapp got to talking about the Coulee, a deep canyon, fifty miles long, which runs southerly from the Columbia River in north central Washington. Donaldson remarked that it was cool in Ephrata in comparison with the Coulee, where the scorching sun's rays beat against the high rock walls.

"Whatever made the Coulee?" Clapp asked, repeating a question white men had been asking since the first of them saw the awesome chasm.

Donaldson told him what he had learned from a geologist friend.

One hundred thousand years ago, give or take a few millennia, glaciers of the ice age had covered the country now sweltering in the summer sun. A great glacier dammed the gorge through which the Columbia River ran. As ice above the blockade melted, the gorge became a great lake, eventually overflowing the banks. Since it could not follow its normal course, the river made a new bed for itself, scouring out the channel which now was the dry Grand Coulee.

As the ice age drew to a close, ever-increasing volumes of water poured into the Coulee. At one place the river, in its new channel, dropped 400 feet over a cliff one and one-half miles wide, forming a cataract the like of which the world does not know today. This is the cliff now called Dry Falls.

The glacier in the old bed of the Columbia was vulnerable, also, to the returning warmth. Gradually it melted. Then, with a swoosh, the river poured through, carrying the rocks and silt, which had helped form the dam, down the original course of the stream.

The Columbia remained in its old bed. The new one, the Grand Coulee, would stand for thousands of years dry and deserted.

Suddenly, Billy Clapp, who was as sharp as he was amiable, was struck by an idea that was to transform a large part of the state and engage his own and the efforts of many other people for the next twenty years.

"Hey!" he exclaimed as Donaldson finished his story. "If ice could dam the Columbia and fill the Coulee with water, why couldn't we do the same? Then we could irrigate the whole Big Bend country!"

The great expanse of land contained within the big bend of the Columbia needed water desperately. The soil of pulverized lava was rich, but not enough rain fell on it to make farming practical. Ranchers had moved in many years before and for a time produced amazing wheat crops. But the moisture in the soil was soon used up and not enough rain fell to replenish it.

Many of the farmers had abandoned their homesteads. Around the tumbled-down farm buildings sagebrush and rattlesnakes replaced the grain and the homesteaders. Several schemes for getting water to the land had been considered in recent years, but the Columbia was thought to be too far down in its canyon for its water to be available.

Possibly nothing would have come of Billy's impulsive idea, if Rufus Woods, editor of the *Wenatchee World,* hadn't come to Ephrata a few days later in search of advertisements and news. A go-getting booster for his part of the state, Woods traveled over the wide, sparsely settled area in a Model T Ford equipped with a built-in typewriter.

He happened to meet Donaldson on the street.

"Any news?" asked the eager editor.

"Nah, awfully dull around here lately," the mining man replied. Then he thought of his conversation with Clapp.

"Say, you might get a story from Billy Clapp," he said. "He's got a real big idea!"

On July 18, 1918, a headline stretched across the front page of the *World.* It read:

FORMULATE BRAND NEW IDEA FOR IRRIGATION GRANT, ADAMS, FRANKLIN COUNTIES, COVERING MILLION ACRES OR MORE.

Woods told of Billy's inspiration in considerable detail. He also revealed that the Grant County commissioners had sent the county engineer to check on it from an engineering standpoint.

That was a fact. Clapp, excited by his brain storm, had asked Norval Enger, deputy county engineer, to take a look at the Coulee and the river at that point to determine if a dam might be feasible. Enger said that Charlie Duncan, his boss, would have to authorize such a project, and Duncan in turn passed the buck to the county commissioners. But Billy got them to agree to let Enger take a look when he was up Coulee way on a road project, even though the Coulee was outside

Grant County.

Some time later Enger reported that the dam would have to be over 550 feet high, an unprecedented engineering feat. The report was filed without further consideration.

Woods' story was ridiculed by practically everyone, except some men in Ephrata and in a few other hamlets of the arid basin. The *World* didn't print another story on the subject for several months.

The idea might well have died right there if Jim O'Sullivan had not returned to town. He first saw the Columbia River in 1906 when, as a lawyer of thirty, he came west with his bride, Pearl, to start a practice. But Seattle, where the young couple planned to settle, had too many lawyers already. So Jim turned to construction work, having had experience in that line. His father was a contractor in Port Huron, Michigan, and the tall, slim young graduate of the University of Michigan had run the business for a couple of years during his father's illness.

In the fall of 1909, he took the Great Northern train to Ephrata where he rented a horse to ride twenty miles to Moses Lake. There he meant to look at some land which a girl had told him could be bought for $1500. He discovered that the irrigation project promoted by the girl's father was a scheme to obtain land around the lake through apparent fraud. Instead of buying the land, O'Sullivan remained to fight the speculators in the courts.

He established a law office in Ephrata on the same street where Billy Clapp had his. The two men became good friends. Jim won his case, after many months of legal conflict. Then he bought a large tract of land at the lake and installed a modern pumping station and irrigation system. He was $40,000 in debt when the land boom broke in 1914.

That same year, Jim's father took ill again, so he went

back to Port Huron to run the business. The elder O'Sullivan
died in 1915, and Jim remained in Michigan to manage the
contracting firm.

Jim did well at contracting, winning several large contracts
during the war and postwar construction boom. From these
substantial profits he was able to pay off some of his debts on
the Moses Lake pumping project. Had he abandoned that
scheme, as his father had advised him to do, and remained in
Michigan he might well have become an extremely wealthy
man.

But the tall, slender lawyer-builder, now in his early
forties, felt a responsibility to the people who had settled at
the lake on the strength of his irrigation project. He was hopeful, too, that the land he owned would once again become
valuable. So he hung on and in the spring of 1919 returned
to Washington to defend himself against a lawsuit arising
from the Moses Lake project.

It was a journey that was to change his entire life and the
life of the Pacific Northwest. But Jim had no premonition
of what was to come when he stepped off the train at Ephrata.

Although Billy Clapp's brain storm had lain dormant for
nearly a year, irrigation of the Big Bend country was still on
everybody's mind. E. F. Blaine, an irrigation man from the
Yakima Valley, had an inspiration about the same time as
Billy had his. He proposed to dam the Pend Oreille River at
Albeni Falls, in Idaho, and run the water 130 miles through
a system of canals, tunnels and siphons to the dry country of
eastern Washington.

Spokane interests took to Blaine's idea at once. His ditch
would pass close to the city, and in winter, when the water
was not needed for irrigation, it could be used to run the
generators of the private power plant that had grown up by
the Spokane falls. Water for hydroelectric generation was

scarce in the winter months when precipitation in the mountains took the form of snow that piled up instead of running off.

The "gravity men," as they became known, wasted no time in persuading the legislature to appropriate $100,000 for a survey of the proposal. The newly appointed Columbia Basin Survey Commission held its first meeting in Spokane in March, 1919, a month before Jim O'Sullivan stepped off the train at Ephrata.

Meanwhile, Billy Clapp's vague scheme for duplicating the ice age had undergone some revision. A dam high enough to make the Columbia flow over its banks into the Coulee would have flooded a great part of southern British Columbia. So in the spring of 1919 Ole J. Kallsted, who had lived in Ephrata but whose home was now in Olympia, wrote to Senator Miles Poindexter saying that a dam need not be that high. A canal could be dug to let the water into the Coulee, he suggested, or the water could be pumped into the Coulee by using some of the great quantities of power that would be produced by a lower dam.

This was the scheme the engineers eventually settled upon, and, quite naturally, the proponents of the dam became known as the "pumpers." Since the dam would produce public power in unprecedented amounts, the battle between the pumpers and the gravity men became part of the bitter public-versus-private power conflict which raged then and which has not entirely subsided to this day.

However, in April, 1919, when Jim O'Sullivan returned to Ephrata, the battle had not even begun. Few paid any attention to Billy Clapp's fantastic brain storm. It had just flared up momentarily in the *Wenatchee World* and the *Grant County Journal* and then subsided.

O'Sullivan retained Clapp as his lawyer in the suit he had come west to defend. Undoubtedly, the old friends discussed Grand Coulee as well as the damage action. In any event, Rufus Woods found the contractor from Michigan full of the subject when he ran into him at Quincy.

The Wenatchee editor told O'Sullivan how he had been unmercifully ridiculed since his story on Grand Coulee appeared the previous year. He had been unable to get a contractor to say whether or not the idea was feasible. Would Jim, as an experienced builder, take a look at the project and, if he found a dam possible, write an article for the *World?* Jim said he would.

Woods, however, did not wait for O'Sullivan's considered opinion. He hurried back to Wenatchee and wrote a story quoting the contractor as saying a dam was not only possible but "perfectly feasible," and added that a dam would "yield untold electric energy, as great as a number of Niagaras." This energy would not only pay for the dam, the story claimed, but would electrify railroads, factories and heat thousands of homes.

Even though Woods had reported his opinions before he could obtain the supporting evidence, Jim went through with his survey. Accompanied by Norval Enger, he reached the head of the Coulee and triangulated a likely site, the same one finally selected by Bureau of Reclamation engineers. O'Sullivan and Enger found that the river was 600 feet below the rim of its canyon at that point and that the canyon itself was approximately a mile wide.

From a book, *Principles of Irrigation Engineering,* by F. H. Newell and Daniel William Murphy, bought in Seattle, O'Sullivan learned that theoretically there is no limit to the size of a masonry dam. As with ships, the authors pointed out, each decade appears to see the ultimate size for a dam, but this is quickly surpassed by the next design.

"It is merely a question of using enough material properly put together, the size being governed by the relation between the cost and the value of the result," the book asserted.

O'Sullivan realized that here lay the crux of the Big Bend irrigation question. In a series of articles for the *World*, he stressed the electric energy a dam would produce. The relation of value to cost made a dam far superior to the gravity system, he contended.

O'Sullivan sent clippings of his articles to Arthur Powell Davis, director of the Reclamation Service. Davis asked the state Columbia Basin Survey Commission to investigate the possibility of building a dam at Grand Coulee. Engineers of the commission made an appointment with O'Sullivan to show them the proposed damsite. But when he pointed it out to them and tried to answer their questions, they laughed at him.

In July Jim had to return to Michigan to look after his contracting business. But he remained interested in the Coulee. A letter from him to Billy Clapp, in which he cited favorable opinions of eastern engineers and gave estimated cost figures for the project, was published in the *World* in June, 1920.

The Coulee proposal received a severe setback the following month, however, when the Columbia Basin Survey Commission made its report to the governor. The Commission supported the gravity system without qualification. In an appendix to the report, the commission labeled as unfeasible a dam in the Columbia at Grand Coulee, even a 180-foot dam which would produce just enough power to pump the water into the Coulee.

The commission questioned the presence there of a proper foundation for even so small a dam. And, anyway, they pointed out, the Bulwer-Lytton Treaty of 1846 provided that navigation on the Columbia River to the sea should be "free and open to the Hudson's Bay Company and to all British subjects trading with the same." A dam in the Columbia, unless it were equipped with exorbitantly costly navigation locks, would violate the treaty, the experts declared.

The "gravity boys" greeted this report with elation. Banquets were held in several towns to celebrate the victory. A tour of the Pend Oreille gravity project was conducted by the Spokane Chamber of Commerce.

In Ephrata, there was no celebrating—only deep gloom. But the "pumpers" were not licked yet. Meeting in Billy Clapp's little office on a hot summer night in 1920, they decided to ask Jim O'Sullivan to come west again and help them. Not only was he a builder and lawyer, who knew how to get and marshal the facts, but also he was an excellent writer and speaker. Jim could make Coulee appear to others as the great project they themselves were sure it was.

Jim came, expecting to spend a couple of weeks, but remained three months. He began at once to tear down the report of the survey commission. First he pointed out that the treaty with Great Britain did not preclude the building of a dam in the Columbia. Its "free and open" provision concerned legal rights; British subjects were merely to have the same rights as Americans.

Then he visited the Columbia River himself, determining from his own observations that the formations promised bedrock not far below the bottom of the river bed. A Seattle engineering firm confirmed his observations. Instead of being 200 feet below the river bed, as opponents of the dam insisted, bedrock would be reached within fifty feet, the firm declared. Jim obtained a mass of other material to help him refute the foes of the dam. That summer he wrote fifteen articles for the *World*, stirring the Big Bend's enthusiasm to a high pitch.

O'Sullivan sent a report on his findings to Director Davis of the Reclamation Service. And when Davis came west in September to address the Northwest Irrigation Congress in Seattle, the Ephrata group persuaded him to look at the damsite.

"Marvelous, marvelous!" Davis exclaimed as he, O'Sullivan and a few others who had driven up from Soap Lake looked across the broad canyon of the Columbia. The engineer, after studying the rock outcroppings in the canyon, agreed that bedrock was only fifty or sixty feet below the bottom of the river. By all means, he said, core drillings should be made to determine definitely the foundations available for a dam.

The Ephrata "boys" were elated. On Billy Clapp's typewriter, O'Sullivan pecked out a story for the *World* reflecting their high spirits. It began:

Friday, September 24, 1920, will prove to be historic in the history of Grant County, and, indeed, the whole State of Washington. The greatest living authority on dams and reclamation then declared emphatically that the construction of the proposed dam on the Columbia River at the head of the Grand Coulee is perfectly feasible from an engineering standpoint.

Colonel Hugh Cooper, who had built the famed Keokuk Dam on the Mississippi and had plans for invading the northwest power field, said much the same thing in November when he stopped off to see the damsite.

"It is alluring—most alluring!" the renowned dam builder declared after Paul Donaldson pointed it out to him. He expressed the opinion the dam project could be built at half the cost of Pend Oreille and could be maintained for even less than half the cost.

Before Colonel Cooper arrived O'Sullivan had gone back to Michigan to look after his contracting business. But he had arranged for the inspection and he remained intensely interested in Grand Coulee during the next nine years while he stayed on in Michigan. He was constantly writing articles and letters, protesting moves of the Spokane group and urging the development at Grand Coulee.

The statements of Davis and Cooper were a blow to the gravity-system supporters. So not to be outdone in big names, they got the Columbia Basin Commission to hire the most famous engineer of all to come out and take a look at the situation. He was General George Goethals, who had built the Panama Canal. The general asked a fee of twenty-five thousand dollars. Fifteen thousand was paid from state funds. Contributors in Spokane made up the balance. General Goethals reported in favor of the gravity system.

For several years thereafter the Grand Coulee dream faded into almost total eclipse. Its backers had no money. The gravity group, on the other hand, was well financed. It maintained a lobby in Washington, D.C., and entertained visiting congressmen and others in the Northwest, stressing the advantages of the Pend Oreille plan. They hardly deigned to mention the dam, now forgotten by most people.

The pumpers, however, were not entirely inactive. They managed to stir up sentiment in Idaho and Montana against taking water from Lake Pend Oreille to irrigate the thirsty acres of Washington.

Billy Clapp was sitting in a barber chair in Sandpoint, Idaho, one day when he mentioned casually that if the gravity system were built it would back up the waters of the lake and flood the town. The alarmed barber spread the word and that evening Clapp was asked to speak to a group of townspeople.

Water at Flathead Lake in Montana also would be impounded and would flood considerable farm land. The legislatures of both Idaho and Montana eventually passed laws prohibiting the taking of water from their states.

But despite such negative successes, the Grand Coulee brain storm remained dormant through most of the nineteen twenties.

Early in 1929, O'Sullivan returned to Ephrata for good. Running the contracting business had impaired his health, which never was good. Litigation among the heirs of his father had used up much of his resources. But he had managed to pay off all his debts, including those involved with the Moses Lake irrigation project, and still had enough left to provide for Pearl and their three children. They went to New Jersey to live with relatives while Jim sought better health in the Far West.

But he came back to no rest cure now. The tall, skinnier-than-ever contractor-lawyer was fifty-two, but he retained the fighting spirit of his youth. He tore into the Columbia Basin case and the public-private power battle like a bulldog. He was named executive secretary of the Columbia River Development League, organized by twenty-nine citizens at Ephrata on June 3, 1929. The group had a high-sounding name and high purpose—to promote Grand Coulee Dam—but it had almost nothing else. In the next few years, Jim O'Sullivan was to travel widely, fighting for the dam, but always doing so on a shoestring.

Looking back, his old friends of the Columbia Basin wonder how he survived, or how he managed to support his family. Mrs. Ed Southard, wife of one of the dam's stout supporters, ran a hotel in Ephrata. She gave Jim a room there for very little money. Billy Clapp provided a desk in his office. Jim had only one suit of clothes and often ate only one meal a day. His health, instead of improving, became worse. For months he suffered from a facial eruption, undoubtedly from overwork and from malnutrition. In summer, when Clapp's office became unbearably hot during the day, O'Sullivan worked until three or four o'clock in the morning, pounding out his propaganda for the dam.

The tall, rumpled man got around the Big Bend country in an old automobile donated to the cause by Billy Ragless of Quincy. For gasoline to operate the car, Jim depended on contributions.

One day, after talking on the Coulee project to a group in Ephrata, Jim announced that he must be at Omak the next day to give a similar talk. He passed the hat and collected two dollars and a half, enough to take him and Joe Niles there. In Omak they persuaded a garage man to donate enough gasoline to get them back home.

Among those who should receive credit for bringing the Grand Coulee campaign to a successful conclusion are a lot of "little fellows" who made regular contributions of one to ten dollars to the champion of their cause. Several Coulee City, Hartline and Almira residents, as well as men and women of other communities, gave Jim small sums whenever possible. Mrs. Tillie Abelson, a widow who ran a bakery in Ephrata, was one of the most faithful contributors. Dollars, however, were mighty scarce in the Big Bend country as the great depression deepened.

It was difficult, too, to maintain enthusiasm for what appeared to be a lost cause. Jim managed to keep hope alive by constantly talking about Grand Coulee. His earnestness and sincerity made a deep impression on his audiences.

One day when things looked really black, O'Sullivan addressed a regular meeting of the Ephrata Chamber of Commerce (the cost of the meal was twenty-five cents). When he

222 - BUILDERS OF THE NORTHWEST

had finished his talk, one of the men rose and addressed the chairman.

"We might as well forget the Grand Coulee Dam and make up our minds that we will never be anything but a little wheat town," he said.

Jim jumped up, with tears running down his cheeks. "Fellows," he implored, "I know you're all discouraged. So am I. But let's just hang on another thirty days, and if we don't get a break during that time even I'm willing to quit."

The chamber decided to hang on, and the breaks began to come.

The biggest of these was the release late in 1931 of the Army Engineers' 308 Report. It surveyed the irrigation, navigation, flood control and power potentials of all major rivers in the country. The section dealing with the upper Columbia River, compiled under the district engineer, Major John S. Butler, recommended construction of the Grand Coulee Dam! And no trifling small dam, either! The Corps of Engineers said it should have a pool level 354.6 feet above low water, creating a lake stretching 151 miles to the Canadian border. And its installed power capacity should be 1,575,000 kilowatts.

This was just the kind of dam the Ephrata group had proposed. And to Jim O'Sullivan's delight the Army Engineers figured the economics of Columbia Basin irrigation just as he himself had in his early articles for the Wenatchee *World*.

The cost of the Pend Oreille gravity system, the engineers declared, would be about $400 an acre for the land watered. At Grand Coulee the cost would be $150.76. But sale of power from the generators would make the actual cost to the farmers only $85 an acre.

This was a tremendous victory for the "pumpers" and for the man who had starved and scrimped to lead the fight. But an Army Engineers' report, ten inches thick, did not ensure the dam's being built. Congress must provide the money, and money was just as scarce in Washington, D.C., as it was in the state of Washington.

There was a lot of fighting still to be done before the huge concrete slab would be laid across the Columbia and the sage-brush-covered and rattlesnake-infested land turned green. Jim O'Sullivan redoubled his efforts, now that victory was in sight.

In 1932 Franklin D. Roosevelt made Grand Coulee and Bonneville Dam on the lower Columbia near Portland an issue in his campaign against President Herbert Hoover. He promised the voters of the Pacific Northwest that both dams would be built if he was elected. After his victory, however, Congress authorized only Bonneville Dam. President Roosevelt too appeared to have cooled off on the Columbia Basin Irrigation Project and the dam that would supply the water for it.

There were, to be sure, sensible-sounding arguments against Grand Coulee. Some four hundred million dollars for the dam and the vast system of canals was a tremendous sum to spend in a depression. Besides, the New Deal was already destroy-ing surplus farm produce to improve the prices received by farmers. Under those circumstances it would be folly, critics declared, to bring more cropland into production.

So Senator Clarence Dill of Washington went to the White House and argued with the President about leaving Grand Coulee out of the multibillion-dollar public-works program. The President offered a compromise.

"Let's build a low dam and make some cheap power for a few years," said F.D.R. "When the depression is over we can finish the dam and start the irrigation project."

The Bureau of Reclamation then commenced work on a

small dam, and Senator Dill was told that the foundations would be substantial enough to hold a higher dam some time in the future. This was small comfort to the "pumpers." A small power dam would not water the dry acres of the Columbia Basin. Obviously Jim O'Sullivan, Rufus Woods, Billy Clapp and all the others had a job cut out for them if victory were not to turn at the last minute into defeat.

In the summer of 1934, President Roosevelt and Harold Ickes, Secretary of the Interior, visited the damsite. O'Sullivan saw to it that at intervals along the route of the presidential caravan people were stationed with large signs. "We want the high dam!" the signs fairly screamed at the Chief Executive and at Ickes.

After seeing the damsite—and reading the signs—Ickes was convinced that the high dam should be built. The President became convinced, too, before long. Then the pumpers got western congressmen to use their influence. O'Sullivan, naturally, was in the forefront of this political battle.

In June, 1935, the Bureau of Reclamation was ordered to scrap the plans for the low dam and to build the high one instead. Soon thousands of workers were on the scene, moving mountains of earth and pouring ten and one-half million cubic yards of concrete. On October 4, 1941, the first power was delivered from the first of Grand Coulee's many giant generators.

But the pumpers had to wait yet awhile for the Coulee to be filled. The Japanese attack on Pearl Harbor put the United States into the war just two months after the first power delivery. The irrigation project must stand still while the country built planes, ships and guns—even atomic bombs in the lower reaches of the basin. But the power from Grand Coulee made these achievements possible. There was no doubt now about who would buy all that power—a question that had been raised often while the pumpers were fighting for Billy Clapp's brain storm and while the dam was under construction.

After the war, work was resumed on the irrigation project. The giant pumps began sending their cascades of water into the Coulee. The ice age bed of the Columbia was back at work. The water actually began to flow through the canals in 1952.

Now the basin is green, its once-arid land laid out in neat squares on which stand new, freshly painted houses and barns. The dusty, little hamlets have grown into substantial towns, fine homes and modern business blocks replacing the frame structures that Jim O'Sullivan had found there in 1909.

The Columbia Basin Project contains several lesser dams which contain and control the water as it flows in various directions from the Coulee. One of these received the not very fancy name of "Potholes." This dam forms the Potholes Reservoir, which lies just to the south of Moses Lake where Jim O'Sullivan first became interested in irrigation 'way back in 1909.

On September 28, 1948, Potholes Dam became O'Sullivan Dam.

Secretary of the Interior Julius Krug flew out from Washington on the twenty-seventh. The governor and several congressmen came from the state and national capitals. Newspapers in several cities printed laudatory editorials about the bulldog of Grand Coulee. Senator Magnuson was toastmaster at the banquet in Ephrata that night. Pearl O'Sullivan sat proudly at the head table with her husband (she had a home with him at last) as Secretary Krug praised Jim and his work.

Next morning, under blue, sunny skies, a delegation from

Moses Lake called for Krug and O'Sullivan at the Bell Hotel in Ephrata. The caravan headed southeast across country along much the same route Jim himself had ridden on horseback thirty-nine years earlier. The schoolchildren of Moses Lake, assembled in front of their buildings, cheered the old man now as he rode by.

Secretary Krug was the main speaker at the dedication ceremonies at the O'Sullivan Dam. The secretary reviewed Jim's long association with the Columbia Basin Project.

"He insists that Rufus Woods, Billy Clapp and many others deserve a major share of credit," said Krug. "That credit is being given them today, Jim, but I want these people out here to remember the nickels and dimes given by thousands of persons during those dark days of the twenties when you spoke yourself voiceless time and again in begging for support for the project. . . .

"Jim, in officially naming this great dam in your honor today we are trying to repay you for the things you have done. . . . It is the first on the project to be named after a man. It required an act of Congress to do it, Jim, but when the congressmen heard about your unselfish devotion for this great development, there wasn't a bit of hesitation in naming the fourth longest dam in the nation after you. . . . Today it is a dam in the desert. Tomorrow it will be a dam in a land of plenty."

The thin, old man—he was seventy-two—wept as he responded to the speech by urging that no effort be relaxed until the entire project was completed.

No one knew then that after the banquet the preceding night Jim had suffered a severe attack, a not uncommon occurrence in recent years, as his health worsened. He was taken to the hospital, but insisted on leaving his bed to attend the ceremonies in his honor. Then after receiving the accolades of high government officials and his more humble fellow citizens, Jim underwent two major operations. On February 15, 1949, he died in Spokane, with his family at his bedside.

Typical of the eulogies his death brought forth was this comment in the *Grant County Journal:*

It is given to few men to leave such an enduring monument to their lives. Jim's monument is more than a gigantic concrete structure called the Grand Coulee Dam; it is more than the O'Sullivan Dam named in his honor; it is more than the miles of transmission lines, huge canals, and other engineering works—his monument is the hope and promise of a finer and better life which the completed project will bring to the thousands of families who will settle on the land.

The man who wrote that eulogy, Herbert Jenkins of Ephrata, recently added another sentence in reminiscing about the bulldog of Grand Coulee.

"It is highly significant that even in the face of powerful and violent opposition, Jim's personal integrity was never questioned."

To be remembered in such terms is no small monument in itself.

EPILOGUE

The Pacific Northwest has changed a great deal since Grand Coulee Dam was built. Hundreds of thousands of people came west during World War II to build ships on the Columbia River and on Puget Sound. The need for bombers and transport planes caused Seattle's Boeing aircraft plant to grow tremendously. Thousands more were enlisted to build and operate a supersecret establishment on the arid plain of southeast Washington. The uranium processed there made possible the country's first nuclear bombs.

The newcomers remained after the war, and others came to join them. When the war industries closed down, employment for the greatly enlarged population became a problem. It was solved by building more dams on the Columbia and its tributaries to provide low-cost power for metal, chemical and other types of manufacturing. Since Grand Coulee a score of dams have been built on the main stem and its branches. Yet the demand for power exceeds the supply and atomic energy has been called upon to supplement the hydro plants.

In the dam-building process, several new irrigation projects have been developed. Also the Columbia and Snake rivers have become a series of slack-water pools where barges ply without interference from the rapids and falls that harassed Captain Ainsworth and his steamboat contemporaries. The floods that once caused serious damage on the Willamette and other streams have been brought under control.

Multilane freeways now strike straight across the country and over the mountains where the men and women in this book wound tortuously around obstructions. Today's motorist can drive as far in an hour as our trailblazers sometimes went in a week. Jet airliners, many built in the Northwest, cover in an hour as great a distance as ox teams plodded in a month.

Yet despite these changes, the region retains many of its pioneer aspects. The Columbia River is still the principal outlet for the wheat produced in eastern Washington, eastern Oregon and Idaho. Modern highways and three transcontinental railroads cross the Cascade Mountains to Puget Sound, as Henry Yesler and the other early settlers had foreseen. But the flow of grain down the river, by barge, rail and highway has not been stopped. This fact underlies recurring attacks and counterattacks on the freight-rate structure. However, regardless of the river, the greatest growth of population and industry has occurred by the deep water of Puget Sound. If the British could have retained that section of the Northwest, Canada today would have been a much richer and larger nation.

Though a million people now reside in the Northwest for every thousand counted a century ago, the region is still sparsely settled, comparatively speaking. Much land remains unplowed or unpaved and this will continue to be true even when, as some predict, a solid city 400 miles long stretches from the head of the Willamette Valley, through western Oregon and Washington and into British Columbia. Fortunately much of the land can be used only for growing trees and some of the sagebrush-covered areas will never be accessible for irrigation.

When a person drives today over some wide highways, that follow closely the old trails, he may catch a glimpse of deep ruts dug a hundred years ago by the wheels of prairie schooners. And, in some places, if he walks a few hundred yards from the highway, he will find himself on an arid plateau or in a deep forest almost unchanged since the mountain men first set foot there. But, of course, he need fear no lurking Indians.

It is an eerie pleasure to stand on a spot where in all probability no human being has ever stood before. Yet that is possible in the wilderness areas of the national parks and national forests that have been set aside in perpetuity as they were when only Indians lived here. And to do this will be just as possible a hundred years from now as it is today. Even the forests not segregated as wilderness will remain; for both public and private timber owners have adopted sustained-yield programs that balance the removal of trees with new growth.

But it is not only in physical appearance that the Northwest retains much of its old flavor. The pioneer spirit also remains strong. Dreams and ambitions are not much different today from those that motivated the people of this book.

Some present-day ventures, like those of the pioneers, are extremely small at their inception. An example is that of the two Portlanders who started a basement workshop to make electronic equipment and now employ several thousand men and women in a vast complex of factories. Other undertakings are almost fantastically ambitious, like the dam-building program of the Grant County, Washington, Public Utility District. This thinly settled county, where the Grand Coulee dream blossomed, is second only to the United States government in building dams and generating power. Some ideas are revolutionary, like that of hauling logs out of the forests by helicopter. This is a long step indeed from the skidroad.

The French have a saying, "The more things seem to change, the more they remain the same." This applies in many respects to the Pacific Northwest.

ACKNOWLEDGMENTS

I am indebted primarily to my good friend, Mr. Stewart H. Holbrook, who urged me to undertake this book and then drew on his own vast experience and knowledge as a writer of popular history to help me get started.

Our first task was to select a dozen men and women, representing various sections of the Pacific Northwest and different periods of the region's development. Mr. Holbrook and I spent several hours in his study going over possible subjects, much as we might have riffled through a giant album or scrapbook. We passed over many of the better-known explorers, politicians and other history makers, looking in the main for the colorful but otherwise ordinary people who are the real builders of any country. Now and then, figuratively, a dim daguerreotype or a sharp steel engraving caught our eyes and we jotted down another name on our list.

However, to translate mere names into three-dimensional people with distinctive character traits, ambitions and other motivations would have been impossible without the work of scores of men and women who had written earlier about these same persons. I have borrowed heavily from the authors whose names are listed in the bibliography. Though such brief mention cannot properly express my indebtedness to them, I am hopeful many of the readers of this volume will feel inclined to read more about the builders of the Northwest in the books here noted.

The Portland Public Library, which has an extensive collection of books about the Northwest, was my principal source of material. The Oregon Historical Society provided another rich field in its files and quarterly where, over a period of many decades, virtually every aspect of pioneer life has been described. I also had access to the files of *The Oregonian*, which go back to 1850. The writings of Mr. Harvey Scott, for many years editor of that newspaper, were especially helpful. These have been conveniently compiled by Mr. Scott's son, Leslie, in his six-volume *History of the Oregon Country*. Many friends lent me books from their private libraries.

Mrs. Evelyn Sibley Lampman, whose stories based on northwest history have enchanted thousands of young readers, kindly let me use her notes on Pete French and the cattle country. Excerpts from the trial transcript, in possession of Mr. Herbert Lundy, were invaluable in separating fact from legend in the French case.

Mr. Ellis Lucia, another Northwest writer, graciously shared his material on Captain Ainsworth. Mr. Richard G. Magnuson, an attorney-at-law in Wallace, Idaho, and Mr. W. R. Brainard, editor of the Kellogg, Idaho, *News*, spent much time and effort in helping to run down the story of Noah Kellogg. Mr. Herbert Jenkins of Ephrata, Washington, drew unstintingly from his rich background on Grand Coulee. To these and others, who may have escaped mention only because of a faulty memory, I am forever grateful.

But, above all, my wife Dorothy deserves credit for the completion of this undertaking. Without her help, it could never have been accomplished. She served not only as expert typist but also as researcher and critic. Whatever success I have had in translating names and facts into living beings is due largely to her deep and sympathetic feeling for the human race.

JALMAR JOHNSON
Portland, Oregon

BIBLIOGRAPHY

Allen, Opal Sweazea, *Narcissa Whitman,* Portland, Binfords & Mort, 1959.

Avery, Mary W., *History and Government of the State of Washington,* Seattle, University of Washington Press, 1961.

Barber, Floyd R. and Martin, Dan W., *Idaho in the Pacific Northwest,* Caldwell, Ida., Caxton Printers, 1956.

Beal, Merrill D. and Wells, Merle W., *History of Idaho,* New York, Lewis Historical Publishing Co., 1959, 3 Vols.

Brimlow, George Francis, *Harney County, Oregon and Its Range Land,* Portland, Binfords & Mort, 1951.

Carey, Charles H., *History of Oregon,* Chicago and Portland, Pioneer Historical Publishing Co., 1922.

Clifford, Henry H., *The Westerners' Brand Book, Book Nine,* Los Angeles, Los Angeles Corral, 1962.

Corning, Howard McKinley, *Willamette Landings,* Portland, Binfords & Mort for Oregon Historical Society, 1947.

Denny, Arthur A., *Pioneer Days on Puget Sound,* Seattle, Alice Harriman Co., 1908.

Duniway, Abigail Scott, *Path Breaking,* Portland, James, Kerns & Abbott Co., 1914.

Elliott, T. C., *The Coming of the White Women,* Portland, Oregon Historical Society, 1937.

Evans, Elwood, *History of the Pacific Northwest,* Portland, North Pacific History Co., 1889.

Fargo, Lucile F., *Spokane Story,* New York, Columbia University Press, 1950.

Fee, Chester Anders, *Chief Joseph, The Biography of a Great Indian,* New York, Wilson-Erickson, 1936.

Fuller, George W., *A History of the Pacific Northwest,* New York, Alfred A. Knopf, 1931.

Grant, Fredric James, *History of Seattle, Washington,* New York, American Publishing and Engraving Co., 1891.

Helm, Myra Sager, *Lorinda Bewley and the Whitman Massacre,* Portland, Metropolitan Printing Co., 1951.

Hobson, George C., *Gems of Thought and History of Shoshone County,* Kellogg, Ida., Evening News Press, 1940.

Holbrook, Stewart H., *Far Corner*, New York, Macmillan Co., 1952.

Holbrook, Stewart H., *Holy Old Mackinaw*, New York, Macmillan Co., 12th printing, 1944.

Howard, Helen Addison, *War Chief Joseph*, Caldwell, Ida., Caxton Printers, 1941.

Johansen, Dorothy O., and Gates, Charles M., *Empire of the Columbia*, New York, Harper & Bros., 1957.

Jones, Nard, *The Great Command*, Boston, Little, Brown & Co., 1959.

Lavender, David, *Land of the Giants*, Garden City, N.Y., Doubleday & Co., 1958.

Lucia, Ellis, *The Saga of Ben Holladay*, New York, Hastings House, 1959.

McDonald, Lucile S., *Washington's Yesterdays*, Portland, Binfords & Mort, 1953.

Meany, Edmond S., *History of the State of Washington*, New York, Macmillan Co., 1924.

Mills, Randall V., *Stern-Wheelers Up Columbia*, Palo Alto, Calif., Pacific Books, 1947.

Monroe, Anne Shannon, and Hanley, William, *Feelin' Fine*, Garden City, N.Y., Doubleday, Doran & Co., 1930.

Morgan, Dale L., *Jedediah Smith*, Indianapolis and New York, Bobbs-Merrill Co., 1953.

Morgan, Murray, *Skid Road*, New York, Viking Press, 1951.

Morgan, Murray, *The Columbia*, Seattle, Superior Publishing Co., 1949.

Parrish, Philip H., *Before the Covered Wagon*, Portland, Metropolitan Press, 1931.

Richardson, Marvin M., *The Whitman Mission*, Walla Walla, Wash., Whitman Publishing Co., 1940.

Ross, Nancy Wilson, *Westward the Women*, New York, Alfred A. Knopf, 1944.

Scott, Harvey W., compiled by Leslie M. Scott, *History of the Oregon Country*, Cambridge, Riverside Press, 1924, 6 Vols.

Smith, Robert Wayne, *The Coeur d'Alene Mining War of 1892*, Corvallis, Ore., The College Press, 1961.

Snowden, Clinton A., *History of Washington*, New York, Century History Co., 1909, 4 Vols.

Spooner, Ella Brown (Jackson), *Tabitha Brown's Western Adventures*, New York, Exposition Press, 1958.

Stoll, William T., *Silver Strike*, Boston, Little, Brown & Co., 1932.

Sullivan, Maurice S., *Jedediah Smith*, New York, Press of the Pioneers, 1936.

Sundborg, George, *Hail, Columbia*, New York, Macmillan Co., 1954.

Tobie, Harvey Elmer, *No Man Like Joe*, Portland, Binfords & Mort, 1949.

Vestal, Stanley, *Joe Meek the Merry Mountain Man*, Caldwell, Ida., Caxton Printers, 1952.

Victor, Frances Fuller, *The River of the West*, Hartford, Conn., and Toledo, O., R. W. Bliss & Co., 1870.

Watt, Roberta Frye, *Four Wagons West*, Portland, Metropolitan Press, 1931.

Wolfe, Louis, *Adventures on Horseback*, New York, Dodd, Mead & Co., 1954.

Wood, Elizabeth Lambert, *Pete French, Cattle King*, Portland, Binfords & Mort, 1951.

Wood, Erskine, *Days With Chief Joseph*, Portland, Binfords & Mort, 1951.

INDEX